THE
MOBILE
MARKETING
REVOLUTION

HOW YOUR BRAND CAN HAVE A
ONE-TO-ONE CONVERSATION
WITH EVERYONE

JED ALPERT
FOUNDER AND CEO OF MOBILE COMMONS
WITH STEPHEN FISHBACH

New York   Chicago   San Francisco
Lisbon   London   Madrid   Mexico City   Milan
New Delhi   San Juan   Seoul   Singapore
Sydney   Toronto

1 2 3 4 5 6 7 8 9 0   DOC/DOC   1 8 7 6 5 4 3 2

ISBN   978-0-07-178818-2
MHID   0-07-178818-2

e-ISBN 978-0-07-178819-9
e-MHID   0-07-178819-0

Library of Congress Cataloging-in-Publication Data
Alpert, Jed.
  The mobile marketing revolution : how your brand can have a one-to-one conversation with everyone / by Jed Alpert. — 1st ed.
    p. cm.
  ISBN 978-0-07-178818-2 (alk. paper) — ISBN 0-07-178818-2 (alk. paper)
  1. Electronic commerce.   2. Communication in marketing.   I. Title.
  HF5548.32.A4547   2012
  658.8'72—dc23
                                            2012000526

Figure I.1 Photo by Lemia Bodden.
Figure 3.1 Photos by National Coalition for Safer Roads, Worthy Publishing, and Harriet Rosen.
Figure 4.1 The Mobile Commons platform.
Figure 4.2 A Mobile Commons campaign as seen on an iPhone.
Figure 8.1 Ross Dettman for Nike.

* * *

TO THE MOBILE COMMONS TEAM

CONTENTS

ACKNOWLEDGMENTS v

INTRODUCTION vii

1 WHY MOBILE? 1

2 BEING IN SOCIAL MEDIA IS NOT ENOUGH,
YOU HAVE TO INVITE EVERYONE BACK TO YOUR PLACE 21

3 STEP 1: MAKE THE ONE-TO-ONE CONNECTION 41

4 STEP 2: DISCOVER THE ONE-TO-ONE OPPORTUNITIES 63

5 STEP 3: INSPIRE ACTION 87

6 STEP 4: DEVELOP A LONG-TERM RELATIONSHIP 111

7 USE DATA TO INCREASE CONVERSIONS
BY STREAMLINING USERS' EXPERIENCE
BEN STEIN 139

8 ONE-TO-ONE TRANSFORMS WHOLE COMPANIES 159

9 ONE-TO-ONE TRANSFORMS COMMUNICATIONS
FOR EVERYONE 185

CONCLUSION   211

NOTES   213

INDEX   217

ACKNOWLEDGMENTS

Without the commitment of the amazing businesses and organizations that have partnered with us, nothing in this book would have been possible. Their creativity and trust has pioneered a new and powerful method of communicating. In particular, I would like to single out Becky Bond of CREDO Mobile, who took a risk on us at the very beginning. Also, Benjamin Stein, my cofounder and CTO, who is in every way an equal contributor and the best business partner and friend anyone could hope for.

The awe-inspiring commitment and intelligence of those working at Mobile Commons and their tireless efforts on behalf of our partners and the company are humbling. They have my profound gratitude. Michael Sabat, Gloria Fong, Kewhyun Kelly-Yuoh, and Mal McKay have been there from almost the start, and I thank them for their patience and perseverance.

I thank Laura Nolan, my agent, who had the idea for the book, and Donya Dickerson at McGraw-Hill who agreed to publish it. Stephen Fishbach, who made the book happen, and Greg Lichtenberg, who helped get it started. Brian Hirsch and Steve Brotman at Greenhill/SAVP and Jay Levy at Zelkova Ventures for investing in us in late 2008 while the world financial system was falling apart. Steven Felsher, Bob Kerrey, and Somak Chattopadhyay for their advice and guidance.

Thanks to my parents and sisters, Jane and Sasha, who have learned not to ask too many questions about my job. I hope this helps explain what I do. Finally, Jackie Sohier and Jay Anania, Amanda Antico, and many others for their support.

INTRODUCTION

Martha Stewart had a problem. Her company, Martha Stewart Living Omnimedia, was spending vast amounts of effort to reach customers through magazines, TV, radio, and the web. But its marketers had no way to further engage with these people who were eager to hear from Martha. People tune out the white noise of traditional advertising. Some messages got through, but then the connection was lost. When I met with her representatives, they wanted to know: wasn't there a way to make a more lasting connection?

They'd come to the right place. My company, Mobile Commons, isn't in the business of selling a quick ad hit. We provide the tools to create lasting relationships by building an active database of users who want to be contacted and who even contact our clients on their own. How did we do that for Martha Stewart? We started by thinking about her customers and their needs. What did they want—frequently—that she could offer?

One thing Martha Stewart customers wanted was her guidance and good taste in the kitchen. Like almost everyone, they often find themselves wondering, what should we have for dinner tonight? That became the basis of our "Dinner Tonight" campaign. Across every form of media, Martha Stewart let her audience know that when they weren't sure what to make for dinner, she could help. If they would text "DINNER" to her number, they would receive a recipe idea every day. Those who liked the day's suggestion could text back the word "COOK" and receive a shopping list, an e-mail of the full recipe, and a text message coupon for one of the ingredients.

Was it a good thing for users? Each day, more than 20 percent of the users asked for the recipe of the day—and it was a different 20 percent each time.

Was it a good thing for the sponsors? The coupon redemption rates were often more than 20 times rates for a typical coupon.

Was it a good thing for Martha Stewart? She built an active database of users who wanted be contacted every day, tying together her various media outlets and creating a new sponsorship channel. Martha now had a roster of potential customers who expected to engage with her on a daily basis and discover what she would offer next. Instead of chasing down consumers with traditional advertising, she had them texting her—*asking* to hear from her and seeking out other news and offers about everything else her company does. Instead of settling for one brief contact, she now had an ongoing text conversation with many of her most interested customers.

Old Forms of Communication No Longer Work

The Reform Immigration For America campaign had a different sort of problem. Back in 2007, with an immigration reform bill on the line, the activist organization had watched helplessly as its opponents outdid its supporters in calling and faxing members of Congress—they were beaten by a ratio of 20 to 1. RI4A knew it didn't lack support, but its community organizers were struggling to reach and mobilize supporters into an active political community. Traditional organizing (going door-to-door, calling, sending out letters) wasn't enough in a new communications era in which people missed the old-style messages because they were working longer hours, giving up their landlines, and ignoring unsolicited snail mail. In addition, many supporters of immigration reform could not afford reliable Internet service. Many more changed addresses frequently. How could RI4A reach and mobilize these people in the twenty-first century?

RI4A began to incorporate a mobile call to action in every available form of media. From their website to their radio campaigns, from billboards to T-shirts and handheld placards at live events, the announcement went out: text in the word "JUSTICE" to start a text message relationship with RI4A in English, or "JUSTICIA" to start one in Spanish (see Figure I-1). In a few months, they had built a list of thousands of potential activists. Then they inspired that group to build the list even further by asking friends to join.

At the time, Representative Luis Guttierez of Chicago was introducing a new immigration reform bill, but RI4A was concerned it would get drowned out by the noise of the healthcare debate. Using their new text message list in coordination with traditional and online organizing methods, they invited supporters to host listening parties where they would gather for a phone call with Representative Guttierez. They texted supporters to announce the coming call and to ask them to RSVP for

Figure I.1   **Reform Immigration For America protesters held up signs inspiring the crowd to text in and join their campaign.** (*Photo by Lemia Bodden.*)

the house parties. An amazing 65,000 people attended house parties around the country, listening in on the call and then placing their own calls to their representatives in Congress. Immigration reform had rediscovered its political voice.

Build on What Your Constituents Want

What made these campaigns so successful? Both organizations built integrated multimedia mobile campaigns around *what their constituents wanted*—which they learned by listening to them as individuals. And at the core of their twenty-first century customer relations management systems was something surprising: the humble text message. Why?

First, everyone will read a text. Without a lot of fanfare, SMS (short message service) messaging has become the most popular form of communication in the world. In 2011, it is esti-mated that almost 8 trillion text messages were sent across the globe. In the United States, more than 5 billion text messages are sent *each day*, far more than the number of phone calls. SMS reaches every demographic under age 50 and is growing among older users as well. Adoption is virtually universal; there will soon be more active cell phones in the United States than there are citizens.

While the media tends to focus on "smartphone" apps, SMS messaging has become the *everyphone* app. Ninety-seven percent of phones can receive a text message, and unlike com-mercial e-mail, which is increasingly ignored, open rates for SMS are extremely high. (When was the last time you got a text and didn't read it?) As the *New York Times* put it, the text mes-sage "may be the closest thing in the information-overloaded digital marketing world to a guaranteed read."[1]

It seems as if everyone has a mobile phone and no one leaves home without it.

Yet a message that gets through is only half of the mobile success story. The second reason text-based mobile campaigns succeed is that so many who receive a text are willing to respond. And when they answer with a message of their own, they start an ongoing text conversation with the sender—or, in the case of large organizations, its customer relationship management (CRM) system. Now the company or organization can be in an ongoing, two-way communication with *every one* of its cus-tomers, clients, members, or potential contacts, *one-to-one*. Organizations can track all of the messages from a given cus-tomer, cross-reference them with the customer's other interactions (purchases, inquiries, service calls, and volunteer activities), and use that data to tailor messages and offerings to each individual customer or member in a systematic and quantifiable way.

In the past, such personalization was time-consuming and expensive; you could only provide it to a small number of people. Most businesses have always been one-to-one with their most important customers: for example, managers of gourmet restaurants, like high-end dealers of clothing or antiques, always made it their business to know top customers personally, to remember everything they bought (or even considered with interest), and to contact them with personalized suggestions just for them. ("A very special wine came in this week that I know you would enjoy.") But mobile-based customer relations systems make it possible to maintain that degree of knowledge, flexibility, intimacy, and effectiveness with *every* customer—even every potential customer—and to create high-value relationships that can last, potentially, forever. For the first time, you can be *one-to-one with everyone*.

For a business to succeed nowadays, you need to be one-to-one with your customers, your audience. We've seen it firsthand at Mobile Commons. Our success with nonprofit organizations as varied as the AARP, National Public Radio, the World Wildlife Fund, and the National Association of Realtors caught the attention of the for-profit world, enabling us to make clients of Nike, Johnson & Johnson, Oprah, and Condé Nast, among others.

We help our clients achieve results that neither conventional advertising and marketing firms nor new media alternatives such as Twitter, Facebook, or foursquare can provide. As a result, our business is growing rapidly. We understand that mobile is not just a marketing channel, it's a conversation channel, and the long-term value for organizations of all kinds comes now in developing and sustaining one-to-one conversations. Because we have focused on creating campaigns that are two-way conversational and integrate with other media, we have become the leader in creating mobile communications in campaigns that scale to the needs of the largest businesses and organizations in the world.

Our mobile campaigns succeed because they do for organizations what the Internet was always supposed to do for businesses, but hasn't. Internet and new media technologies were supposed to launch a new age of effective communication, revolutionizing business and organizations of all kinds. Yet while media has been two-way for two decades, and businesses must be "always on," in many ways today's customers and clients are actually harder to reach than before. It's harder, not easier, to get and hold their attention. It's harder, not easier, to establish a brand or maintain its integrity, or to maintain a long-term relationship with the people an organization depends on most. It's no longer enough to put a message in front of as many "eyeballs" as possible, the way it was when there were only three main television channels and a handful of local stores to visit. Today, traditional advertising often feels to customers like nothing more than an annoying interruption, if the audience doesn't find a way to skip it altogether. For all these reasons, there is a growing disconnect between organizations and the audiences they need to reach, from high-end retail to low, from advocacy groups to government agencies.

Use Mobile to Transform Your Existing Outreach

Why hasn't there been a book like *The Mobile Marketing Revolution* until now? Because most people, even in new media, are expecting the wrong kind of change. As each year ends, we see the same articles and features in the media and the blogosphere, asking, "Will next year be the year of mobile?" It's the wrong question. The revolutionary opportunities afforded by integrated mobile campaigns won't take the form of a conventional revolution. Neither mobile nor any new science-fictional technology will rise up to cut the heads off of TV, radio, newspapers, the Internet, social media, and so on to replace them with a new technological regime. The truly revolutionary change comes when mobile approaches are *integrated with existing media*. Every organization today faces a crucial choice and opportunity, but it is not the choice either to do what you've always done or to throw it all away; it's about taking existing strategies and optimizing the one-to-one connection by pairing them with mobile.

It comes down to this. Businesses and organizations of every type and size all face a radically changed world of disaggregated markets and disconnected customers, clients, supporters, and audience. But our clients don't stand by while they lose their connections to customers. They don't give up on one-to-one relationships and bet everything on social media sites. They don't endure endless switching from one technological platform to another. Instead, they meet the challenges of the new media age. This book shows how to use integrated mobile campaigns to build trusted, long-term relationships that will hold even as company needs and technologies evolve.

This book will offer up real-world examples of how companies, government agencies, nonprofit institutions, and organizations of every kind are using mobile to transform their outreach. They're taking all the media channels they currently use—from traditional TV and radio ads to flash widgets and geolocation features—and use it all to draw consumers into an intimate, one-on-one, text-based conversation using the one technology that is with them 24-7, the mobile phone. By the time you've read this book, you'll probably have ideas for how mobile can help your organization. Holding onto customers is more challenging than ever, but success is possible if you have *The Mobile Marketing Revolution*.

WHY MOBILE?

No one expected that text messaging—an internal testing feature included free with every cell phone—would have any commercial applications, let alone that it would become the most widely utilized data application in the world. And even now that text messaging services claim 4.6 billion subscribers, orders of magnitude more than any phone app, business is in danger of underestimating it once again. SMS is as essential for business and organizational users as it already is for individuals. Why? As the Internet and other new media technologies continue to destabilize our established ways of communicating—advertising, public relations, direct mail, customer service, internal corporate communications, and more—text-based mobile campaigns offer a unique solution to the contemporary disconnect, not only restoring lost connections but taking existing relationships to a higher level.

Text messages drive people to action—whether it's voting, clicking a link, seeking out a vaccine, redeeming a coupon, making a phone call, or merely sending in their personal information. These are but a few of the uses that yield outcomes orders of magnitude greater than other forms of communication—and at a significantly lower cost. And yet the story of text messaging has none of the expected trappings of a blockbuster Internet

Age success—no hungry young PhDs working in a Silicon Valley garage, no ultra-high-tech breakthroughs, and no overnight billionaires.

Friedhelm Hillebrand, the German communications researcher who first saw the commercial potential of SMS and settled on its length limit, didn't even conduct market research. Hillebrand was working to come up with a technology that would allow cell phones to transmit and display messages. His initial vision was small: that businesspeople with car phones (at the time, the only kind of cell phone in widespread use) would use SMS as a paging system on the road. Because the cellular networks had limited bandwidth, messages needed to be as small as possible. That's why the first *S* in SMS stands for "short" (SMS stands for "short message service").

Working from home in 1985, Hillebrand reasoned that most of what people really needed to say would probably fit on a postcard, then tried out some sample messages for length on his typewriter. He discovered that these sentences were almost always shorter than 160 characters. "This is perfectly sufficient," he decided, in typically German fashion. "Perfectly sufficient."[1] Satisfied, he used his position as chairman of the nonvoice services committee of the Global System for Mobile Communications to require that all cell phones be capable of sending 160-character messages. Hillebrand owned no stake in this new application, and it never made him rich.

In fact, like many revolutionary technologies, SMS was slow to take hold. The world's first SMS message wasn't sent until December 1992. A 22-year-old engineer named Neil Papworth used his personal computer to text "Merry Christmas" to

Vodafone director Richard Jarvis—the "Hello, Watson" moment of text messaging technology. The first SMS typed on a phone (rather than a computer) was sent the next year, in 1993, by Riku Pihkonen, an engineering student at Nokia. When the mobile providers eventually did set up SMS gateways, they were meant to be used for network notifications—usually, text messages to let customers know they had received a new voicemail.[2] By 1995, customers were sending an average of only 0.4 messages per month.

Before the dawn of predictive typing and pop-up keyboards, texting was a slow and laborious process. Every character had to be entered through multiple taps on the cell phone's keypad. And challenges to digital dexterity weren't the only obstacles holding the new technology back. Part of the reason behind SMS's slow adoption was that, at first, carriers had no consistent way to charge for SMS plans. And why would they promote a new service they had no way of monetizing?

In North America, another hurdle to widespread adoption was that users couldn't text between the wireless carriers. Different cell phone carriers in North America had adopted different wireless standards, and for technical reasons, it was impossible to SMS between them. So if you had a Sprint plan, it was functionally impossible for you to text your friend if she was on the Verizon network. (In Europe, where Friedhelm Hillebrand's GSM was dominant, interoperability was never a concern.) But as mobile phones evolved from an ostentatious status symbol that users lugged around in a briefcase to the convenient nearly pocket-sized device of the early 2000s, the carriers realized that in order for their SMS services to achieve scale, they would need to learn to work together. By May 2002, as the carriers were adopting cooperative standards, about 1 billion text messages were sent every month in the United States.

Just eight years later, in June 2010, U.S. mobile phone subscribers sent 173 billion text messages—an average of more than 600 per person. Globally, about 8 trillion messages were sent in 2011. From a format that carriers couldn't figure out how to monetize, text messaging has evolved into a $200 billion global business.

Text messaging triumphed not by dazzling the world with new technology or by brilliant marketing but by doing what matters most in the Internet Age: it made itself useful to users. It helped them do something they wanted to do, namely, communicate quickly and easily, where and when they wanted to do it.

In fact, many of text messaging's so-called competitors, elaborate applications and sophisticated technologies such as the mobile web, can't replace text messaging exactly *because* of their technical sophistication. Texts have by far the widest reach of any form of communication, making text messaging the most effective way to reach both rich people and poor people and bridge the "digital divide" between the 60 to 70 percent of users who have access to broadband Internet service and the 30 to 40 percent who are "have-nots." Text messages are compatible with almost every type of mobile phone. That's true regardless of whether a person has a "smart" phone, like an iPhone or an Android, or a much simpler "feature" phone, which nowadays is any mobile device more complex than a Styrofoam cup and a piece of string.

Text messaging is also uniquely protected from spam. That means consumers won't reach the point where they distrust messages they've *asked* for because they can't distinguish them from hoaxes and scams. The FCC has ruled that SMS spam messages to cell phones are illegal, under the Telephone Consumer Protection Act and the CAN-SPAM Act, unless the device's owner has explicitly given permission. Wireless carriers have broad powers to stop spammers at the source—much more access than e-mail providers. Anybody can sign up for an e-mail account, after all. Cell phone service, on the other hand, requires book-length contracts in tiny print that nobody actually reads. Those contracts give the carriers the ability to track bulk messaging to its source.

Furthermore, sending an e-mail is free—but sending texts costs money.[3] Even if 99 percent of a spammer's e-mails are blocked by spam filters, they only need to make $1 to turn a profit. But spamming out millions of text messages could mean paying hundreds of thousands of dollars. Even if you had a hundred relatives trapped in Nigerian prisons, requiring just a small cash investment to unfreeze millions of dollars, text spamming just doesn't make financial sense.

Text messaging is more immediate than e-mail. It erases the digital divide. It's spam free. It has faster response rates, higher open rates, and more precipitous growth rates. For these reasons and many more, it represents an evolution in digital communications past the constraints of e-mail. For businesses and other organizational users, it presents the logical next step in their efforts to engage with their audiences, to disseminate information, and to build relationships.

Yet many organizations have been slow to adopt text messaging. If you're in the business of communicating, you want to ply your trade using the most pervasive form of communication that exists. It's almost axiomatic. Yet for some reason, with each successive evolution in technology, some futurists insist that it has limited application. I remember attending meetings in the mid-1990s about the uses of e-mail and other new technologies in which people would wonder, "What sort of organizations will want to use e-mail? Who will want to build websites?" as though these activities were niche tools for special cases.

Of course, looking back now, that's ridiculous. But it's always ridiculous looking back. It's a little harder to have perspective when you're in a moment of rapid technological advancement. In the early days of the telephone, there was a debate over whether or not phone service should reach every household in the United States. Not just *would* phone service expand that broadly—but *should* it. As Columbia Professor Tim Wu writes in his book *The Master Switch*, "[The clientele] of the first Bell monopoly consisted of businesses and rich individuals living in large East Coast cities; Bell was in no hurry to broaden the coverage of its network. . . . Bell's shareholders were monotonously interested in dividends alone." People living in rural areas, particularly in the West, were forced to create makeshift telephone wires of their own, "With nothing but galvanized wire and barbed wire."[4]

The same suspicions and biases held true for electricity in *its* early days. Some people thought electricity made sense for large urban areas but had limited application in rural America. Probably in caveman days, language itself was seen as a nice invention for a select few, but not of much practical application for your ordinary grunter.

Text messaging, as with e-mail, as with the World Wide Web, and as with electricity, makes up the fabric of the way we communicate. It's not an alternative to e-mail, TV, and websites; it's a powerful addition and must be added to any organization's media mix. And if used correctly, it can revolutionize the way that businesses and organizations communicate with their users.

Mobile Extends the Web's Revolutionary Democratization of Information

When I first started working as a lawyer in 1989, at the law firm of Paul, Weiss, Rifkind, Wharton & Garrison LLP, I had a secretary. Assistants and secretaries were pervasive back then. In many cases people had more than one if they were just "that important." That person's job was a lot more complex than just answering your phone calls and taking the occasional memo. Your assistant was a vital information-gathering resource. Whenever you needed background data, research, or an outside perspective, you turned to her (or him, but usually her) to track the information to its source. Cataloging and accessing information wasn't some peripheral duty. As today, industries ran on information. And in the 1980s, you needed that information curated.

As we all know, personal computing, the web—and particularly hyperintelligent search engines—have completely revolutionized that process. The resources that used to go to tracking down and retrieving information now can be better allocated. In *The World Is Flat*, Thomas Friedman recalls asking Colin Powell "when he realized the world had gone flat:"[5]

> He answered with one word: "Google." Powell said that when he took over as secretary of state in 2001, and he needed some information—say, the text of a UN resolution—he would call an aide and have to wait for minutes or even hours for someone to dig it up for him.
>
> "Now I just type into Google 'UNSC Resolution 242' and up comes the text," he said. Powell explained that with each passing year, he found himself doing more and more of his own research, at which point one of his press advisors remarked, "Yes, now he no longer comes asking for information. He already has the information. He comes asking for action."

Powell's press aide cuts to the crux of the issue: rather than asking for information, Powell can ask for action. When accessing data has become trivial, it doesn't get rid of the need to have an assistant. Instead, it elevates the assistant's role into much more productive work. The web democratizes the flow of information and automates tasks that should be automated. Now your assistant isn't stuck slogging through libraries of ancient legal arcana only available in dusty tomes; now he or she is coming up with creative ways to use it. Friedman writes, "There are a lot more conversations between bosses and staffers today that start like this: 'I know that already! I Googled it myself. Now what do I do about it?'"

In the early 1990s, the *New Yorker* ran a fascinating article about media tycoon Barry Diller.[6] After seven solid years of guiding Fox Broadcasting Company to stellar growth and record profits, Diller was chaffing under Rupert Murdoch's managerial thumb. (Fox, then as now, was a division of Murdoch's News Corporation). "There is only one principal in this company," Diller remembered Murdoch saying. Diller's journey to liberation began, he claimed, when he purchased a PowerBook—one of the first commercially successful laptop computers:

> The machine's allure was that it promised a certain kind of freedom—from secretaries, meetings, memos, press leaks. Diller used it to compose his resignation statement; to fax draft copies of the statement to Murdoch and to his own closest friend, the clothing designer Diane Von Furstenberg [now his wife] to list things he must do before issuing the statement [of resignation from Fox]; to sort from his copious address book the three hundred people he wanted to have received the resignation statement before they heard or read about it; to jot down notions of what he might like to do next and whom he might consult. The PowerBook went with him everywhere. . . . Just as Diller could convert his laptop into a word processor, a fax, a file cabinet, a spreadsheet, a conveyor of commands, or a link to various networks of news or data, so in the next few years, he came to understand, viewers will receive video on demand—be able to watch what they want when they want. With the click of a remote-control or a tele-

phone button, they will summon up movies from the equivalent of a video jukebox. In an instant, they will send for and receive a paperless newspaper, a program they missed last night, a weather report.

To give you some context, this was when CompuServe and Prodigy were still the largest online Internet portals and a young upstart called America Online was making inroads into their dominance. Diller was able to use his laptop to circumvent a whole society's worth of restrictive conventions and mediating structure and gaze directly into the digital future.

Of course, democratizing information for media moguls like Barry Diller or enormously powerful government officials like Colin Powell isn't the *most* inspirational way the web has transformed society. But the web has also made it so that Josh Marshall at *Talking Points Memo* can have the same reach as the *New York Times*. Not only does the web democratize who can access information, but it democratizes *what kind of information can be accessed*. Now, to have an influence on public opinion, you don't need a multimillion-dollar newspaper or television channel behind you. You just need to sign up for a free account with Blogger.

The rise of Salesforce.com and customer relationship management (CRM) software took the democratizing power of the web and extended it into business analytics. Knowing your consumer and satisfying their needs is essential to any successful business. Thus, getting the answers to questions like, "*What* kind of people are purchasing my product?" "*How* often do they make those purchases?" "*Why* are they purchasing?" and "*How* are they using my product?" are invaluable—or, more accurately, extremely valuable—to a business. They can guide advertising, packaging, new product development, and basically every other step in the product's life cycle, from conception to consumption.

But in-depth and accurate market research used to be extremely difficult to obtain. Thus, an entire industry of market research firms developed to track and record that information—and after going through the arduous process of gathering this data, they weren't going to give it away for free. As a result, it used to be that only big consulting firms like McKinsey and huge consumer products corporations like Gillette and Proctor & Gamble were able to get reliable information about their customers. In a competitive marketplace, start-up businesses were inherently at a loss. They just couldn't afford the data.

The advent of CRM software revolutionized analytics. Imagine a very complicated Excel spreadsheet that basically tracks every interaction with every customer or client—or *potential* client. A CRM system is a way for companies to keep track of their sales leads, existing clients, current and past donors—basically to automate and organize the entire business of selling and soliciting. Now people have a way of seeing and reading their own data.

Salesforce, one of the earliest and most widely adopted CRMs, claims that 78 percent of a sales representative's day is spent hunting for information—like the latest presentations or deal updates—rather than actually selling.[7] By centralizing and organizing all that information, suddenly you enable a sales rep to engage with clients more effectively and with a great deal more personalization. Like Colin Powell's press aide, your reps are now able to do more than gather information—they're able to act on it. Your business evolves from being like the manager of the gourmet restaurant who only knows the preferences of his biggest-spending customers to being like IBM with a full complement of market analytics.

Salesforce is just one CRM, focused on one aspect of business—sales. There's a CRM system, or multiple CRM systems, for every type of business or organization imaginable. If you're a nonprofit looking to engage constituents around issues and raise money, Blue State Digital, Blackbaud, Convio, Salsa, and others have been optimized to meet those needs. If you're a healthcare provider or pharmacy, then McKesson might be the right CRM for you. And CRMs are a lot more elegant and powerful than just Excel spreadsheets. Salesforce looks more like a Facebook page where instead of "friends" you have leads. By providing simple ways to organize and share information, CRMs enable small businesses to compete with the resources of big businesses. Conversely, they also enable big businesses to keep an infinity of data sorted and stored, allowing them to have the personalization of a small business.

So the web democratizes information and provides new resources and opportunities for business. That's all old news—it's been written about in book after book. So why all this background information in a book about mobile? The best answer may be another anecdote: this time, about how the mobile phone is transforming the economics of Africa.

Right now, Africa is the fastest-growing mobile phone market in the world.[8] According to Ken Auletta, the number of phones "has grown from fewer than four million in 1998 to more than four hundred million today—almost half the population of the continent."[9] In Kenya, while only a few hundred thousand households have electricity, millions of people have mobile phones.

Mobile has completely transformed the logistics of fishing and farming throughout Africa. Farmers can check crop prices now *before* taking their goods into cities and villages.[10] They can use their phones to look into the upcoming weather. And more and more Africans are using electronic payments through cell phones in lieu of having bank accounts. As the *Christian Science Monitor* reports:

> 80 percent of Zambians, particularly in rural areas, don't have bank accounts. By using mobile banking, farmers are not only able to get paid more quickly and transparently, but they can also use their mobile accounts to send money transfers, buy phone credit, pay school fees for their children, and order agriculture inputs such as fertilizer and seed. Electronic payments also allow them to build up a credit history over time.[11]

Mobile phones also allow healthcare workers in the field to better communicate with their home base hospital—asking for advice or requesting additional medication.

In short, mobile has all the revolutionary power today that the web did 20 years ago—but with even greater reach. Mobile democratizes the information that people can receive and empowers them to communicate with each other. A mobile phone lets you quickly receive and send data—and that data could be anything from a request for healthcare supplies to a cash transfer. As portable and accessible as Barry Diller's laptop was, a mobile phone is lighter, it's more convenient, and it's just as obtainable for a farmer in Kenya as it is for the head of Fox Broadcasting Company.

Mobile Enables a Two-Way Conversation That Lets You Know Your Audience

Mobile communication is also conversational. In many ways, the size restraint that Friedhelm Hillebrand placed on SMS— just 160 characters—has remained its greatest strength. Text messaging demands brevity. That forces both individuals and companies to clarify and simplify their messaging before they hit "send." The corollary is, when you receive a text, you can be assured you're not getting a series of complicated demands requiring hours of your time. You know that whatever pops up on your phone screen is going to be easy to digest and easy to respond to. As a result, the average time before a recipient views a text message is 14 minutes—as opposed to an average wait time of 6.4 hours for e-mail.

When you combine (1) the ability to quickly access data with (2) the ability to reach everybody and (3) mobile's conversational nature, you have an incredibly powerful communications tool.

You also have the potential to be incredibly annoying. When you have the power to gain access to the entire world's pockets, you'd better use that power responsibly. The traditional tactics of broadcast—whether that broadcast is television or direct mail—just don't work anymore. You can't go blasting out your message repeatedly, hoping it catches the ear of 1 percent of your listeners. People have much less tolerance for white noise on their phones. That's why, when the occasional spam message does slip through the wireless carriers' nets, they get immediately alerted to it by angry calls from subscribers.

Fortunately, with an SMS campaign, you don't have to rely on broadcast tactics. SMS allows for a radical type of messaging personalization that no other medium can reach. And it does so by fulfilling the potential of CRM software.

CRM systems work by organizing and streamlining all the data you have about your clients and leads. With mobile, you dramatically increase the amount of data you have available. A good mobile CRM can keep track of every text message sent, every phone call made, and every web link clicked. You can see how one user joined your mobile list, how long he or she spent on the phone with the White House, or how likely that person is to take action.

While that at first blush may seem to raise privacy concerns, you have to remember that every single person who is on your mobile list has given express permission to be there. Most Internet advertising these days is incredibly sneaky. By tracking users' behavior and throwing up ads around it—whether it be Google search terms, Facebook interests, or browser history— Internet advertising today is essentially peeping over users' shoulders and accessing information they never wanted to reveal. Mobile campaigns, on the other hand, aren't installing spyware on users' mobile device or tracking how long they spend on the phone with their moms. Rather, a mobile CRM can assemble extensive profiles of *just* the actions people take within a mobile campaign. Then an organization can use those data and analytics to personalize its messaging.

At the most basic level, companies can track their lead acquisition. They can see what keywords people are texting in to join their campaigns, which allows for A/B testing across multiple different keywords—and it immediately allows you to segment your audience based on interest. Let's say you were running a business that sold pet-care products. You could have one billboard with an adorable puppy asking dog lovers to text in "PUPPY" to your mobile short code. You could have another billboard with an adorable kitten playing with a ball of twine asking cat lovers to text in "KITTY." Right away, you can now immediately segment your users into those who would be interested in cat information or products and those who would be interested in dog-related items. In fact, the ASPCA does exactly that—it has segmented users based on whether they're interested in dogs or cats so that it can make its appeals more compelling.

Our customer Reform Immigration For America, which is mentioned in the Introduction, used this capability to streamline its outreach between English speakers and Spanish speakers. It asked English-speaking users to text "JUSTICE" to its short code if they wanted to get involved in its campaign; Spanish-speaking users were asked to text in "JUSTICIA." That let RI4A easily maintain two separate lists, targeted by language, so nobody gets a message he or she doesn't understand. As we later learned (and I'll be discussing later), reaching out to different English and Spanish lists required deeper cultural understanding than you could find with just Google translate.

A mobile campaign lets you target your messaging around much more than just a keyword. Our system, for example, lets you select any of an infinity of criteria—such as age or gender—with the most frequently used being location. Our commercial customers want to direct users to the closest store. Our political customers want to ask users to attend a local phone bank—or let them know where their polling place is. Healthcare clients want to help users find a flu clinic near them.

Does that sound like the kind of information that could be conveyed through a Google map? It is—if everybody had access to Google maps. But the more salient point is that a Google map relies on the user inputting the search term unprompted. An effective mobile campaign builds two-way conversations between an organization and its audiences. So when the Obama campaign asks you to head to your local phone bank, it's an action that you're inclined to take. Or when the California Department of Health tells you to text in to find the closest flu vaccination provider, it's a top-of-mind activity. After all, you just got a text reminder.

And because a mobile CRM keeps track of every action that a user takes, sometimes you can learn unexpected lessons.

In the Introduction, for example, I wrote about the house parties that the Reform Immigration For America campaign set up in support of Representative Luis Guttierez's national conference call.

Because RI4A thought that hosting a house party was a "big ask," at first it only sent messages out to its most active supporters—as determined by who had made the most phone calls or taken other actions involved with the campaign. Campaign leaders figured that someone who had never made a phone call for the campaign probably wouldn't let people into his or her home.

But when RI4A broadened the ask to the entire list, it found that there wasn't any correlation between having made calls for the campaign and hosting a party. Hosting a party wasn't a big ask—it was just a *different* ask.

We have a tendency to think that there's a linear scale of engagement. People go from being unengaged to doing things that are easy, like sending texts or making phone calls, to doing things that are hard, like organizing house parties or giving money. And to a certain extent, that is true; many organizations are extremely accomplished at moving their members up the "ladder of engagement" from initial contact into passionate support. But as the house parties show, there are also just different kinds of people. The kinds of things that might appeal to one person won't necessarily appeal to another.

Being able to correlate new actions to past actions let RI4A gain new insights into its constituent base. It learned which of its members were active callers and which were willing to open their doors and host a party. Using that knowledge, RI4A can further personalize its messaging in the future.

That hints at the truly revolutionary power of mobile. Through the use of data and analytics, you can turn a national campaign into specific local action.

As a result, SMS has the power—more than any other communications approach, from traditional marketing to social networking—to move customers all the way through marketing's traditional "purchase funnel," from awareness to engagement to sale.

The phone company CREDO Mobile is particularly skilled at that. CREDO has been one of Mobile Commons' most consistently innovative customers. In addition to being a mobile provider, the company is led by progressive political activists—and in a city like San Francisco, where it's based, having a progressive bent is a great way to engage potential customers. That's not to suggest that CREDO is cynical. It's anything but. Rather, in an era of limitless consumer choice, people are more and more making their consumption decisions between nearly equivalent services based on brand values.

In 2007, CREDO wanted to make a public statement and involve San Franciscans in large-scale political satire. CREDO projected a cartoon of former Vice President Dick Cheney on prominent walls across San Francisco and asked passersby to text in and fill his "speech balloon" with their own ideas. Using text-to-screen technology, people could text in and have their words appear inside CREDO Mobile's projection. Simply by texting in, San Franciscans literally could put words in Dick Cheney's mouth. According to CREDO, the project "turned regular blank walls into theaters for people's opinions."[12]

Moreover, when people texted in their ideas, CREDO could respond to them and ask for their e-mail addresses. Right away, engaged passersby become potential business leads. That's just the first step toward CREDO selling them a mobile phone plan.

Whether it's giving money to the Sierra Club or selling a mobile phone, text messaging can turn even the briefest initial interaction into a permanent engaged relationship.

In the next chapter, you'll see how, by building those relationships, mobile can help you realize the potential of your existing social media outreach.

BEING IN SOCIAL MEDIA IS NOT ENOUGH, YOU HAVE TO INVITE EVERYONE BACK TO YOUR PLACE

Imagine you're on a fishing trip. Are you hoping to ride out on the boat, see a lot of fish swimming in the water, and then go home? Of course not. You want to catch some fish. Yet when it comes to "fishing" for customers or any kind of audience, it seems almost everyone is talking about social media. And while social media do offer a huge and well-stocked pond, they just don't bring home the fish.

In 2009, for example, vitaminwater made the dramatic decision to shut down its website, vitaminwater.com, and replace it with a home page on Facebook. The company then crowd-sourced development of a new soft drink to its Facebook fans. As the website iMediaConnection.com describes it:

> Fans were able to vote on flavor, ingredients, packaging, and naming for the new drink, with the person who created the winning name getting a $5,000 prize. The process

started with the flavor creator lab, a Facebook app that crowd-sourced the flavor for the newest vitaminwater, black cherry–lime. Next up, participants completed a series of games and quizzes to determine which vitamins were needed most. . . . fans could [also] submit their own packaging and naming ideas.[1]

The resulting drink, vitaminwater Connect, even put the Facebook logo on its bottle. The company soon declared the campaign a winner. It noted that the number of fans on Facebook had increased from 400,000 to 981,000 in one month—and ultimately reached more than 1.3 million fans by the time the new drink launched.

iMediaConnection.com hailed the campaign as "bold but brilliant," a success that spoke for itself. But success at what, exactly?

Every day another story in the blogosphere and the business press describes companies' promotions that increase the attention they get on social media sites. These campaigns give companies tremendous access to the millions of consumers who populate these sites. But the enormous potential of social media has allowed many of us to lose sight of what Taddy Hall, writing in *Advertising Age*, called the Martha Stewart Rule: "Throw your own party; don't just cater someone else's!" He went on to explain: "If you base your social campaigns in venues you don't control—such as Facebook or YouTube—you may get great 'attendance,' but data show it's hard to convert and retain these party-goers. If your goals are anything beyond building brand awareness, it's better to have a house of your own where friends can find you."[2]

By including Facebook in its expensive advertising campaign, adding the Facebook logo to its new product, and privileging Facebook users over other customers, vitaminwater did far more for Facebook than Facebook ever did for vitaminwater. Yes, the campaign alerted hundreds of thousands of consumers to the new flavor. But how much more did that actually accomplish than a 30-second TV commercial? vitaminwater promoted a party over Facebook rather than catering its own.

The problem here is not that organizations are establishing a beachhead in social networks. It's that they're giving up ground they have earned *by not taking the last step* and reaping the benefit of those networks. Social media can't be a replacement for traditional forms of connection. When you look past the new-media gloss, Facebook, Twitter, foursquare, and so forth are an efficient new means to solve a classic media conundrum: How can we reach a big, general audience?

For the last 60 years, organizations have used television, radio, newspapers, and magazines to reach that audience. Social media are the contemporary answer to the important question, Where the hell is everybody? Social media gather an audience.

But a big, general audience is just the beginning of success. In his recent keynote at Salesforce.com's Dreamforce conference, Eric Schmidt, former CEO of Google and now Google's executive chairman, talked about how the web has empowered—but also limited—activism. "One of the things I learned about the Internet is that everyone feels like they're being heard and nothing changes," he said. "So the good news is—you can be heard. That's no longer the criteria by which activism should be judged. It should be judged based on outcomes."[3] That mantra could apply to almost any other endeavor on the Internet. Companies can't just dive into social media hoping to be heard. They need to think about outcomes.

It's nice to fish in a big, well-stocked pond, but it's not enough to wave at a lot of fish in the water. You need to hook them and reel them in.

How Do You Reel Them In?

The past six years are littered with social media missteps. Hundreds of organizations created social media campaigns with no clear goal that they were trying to achieve. Often, these campaigns ended up generating more negative attention than positive.

In 2006, General Motors launched a contest asking for user-generated videos promoting its new Chevy Tahoe SUV; it was overwhelmed with response videos that mocked the SUV's environmental impact. In 2009, Skittles redesigned its home page to pull directly from social media highlighting the brand.[4] Online pranksters hijacked the effort, pushing content to social media sites that either mocked Skittles or had nothing to do with Skittles at all. Spammers were able to promote their own products directly on the Skittles.com home page merely by sending out a tweet with the #skittles hashtag. In 2010, Nestle got in trouble for deleting comments from its Facebook page that were critical of its use of palm oil, which Greenpeace claims is harmful to the environment.

The problem for these campaigns was not just bad luck in setting off an overwhelming backlash of Internet mob antagonism. By entering into social media for their own sake, campaigns are inherently at risk. Without fully thinking through the goals and protocols of a successful social media campaign, brands open the door to seeing their campaigns hijacked to serve someone else's agenda. Or, as many campaigns have discovered, you simply might not garner any attention at all.

There's even an award for biggest social missteps—the Suxorz,[5] which is like the Razzie of social media marketing. The restaurant chain Denny's won the 2010 award for "Missed Connections" when it used the menus at its 1,500 locations to direct diners to www.twitter.com/dennys. The problem was that Denny's actually didn't own the twitter user name Dennys, so diners who followed that link didn't wind up on the official Denny's Twitter page. Instead, twitter.com/dennys led them to the personal Twitter home page of Dennys Hsieh, a young man in Taiwan, a recent tweet of whose was "網路測試: 目前在光復路上, telnet 會頓, 但是 ftp 還是有 100KB/s ... 這就是 3G 最討厭的地方了, 用 ftp 這種來看其實都還好, 可是 telnet 之類需要即時反應的就會有感覺"—a fairly technical tweet about FTP and 3G in Chinese characters. Not exactly the kind of content that makes someone crave a Grand Slamwich.

My point is not to criticize the low-hanging fruit of social media mistakes. An advertising campaign can go wrong no matter what medium it uses.

And vitaminwater's Facebook campaign is actually an example of a social media *success*. The campaign achieved its goals of gaining Facebook fans and had an overwhelmingly positive media response. Since the initial campaign, vitaminwater's Facebook page has been a model of sustained engagement. The page has featured additional promotions and coupons, and it has an almost daily status update from the team that invites a

user response. For example, on September 4, 2011, vitaminwater posted "milk & cookies. coffee & doughnuts. vitaminwater
& _____?" The company received 1,292 responses, with
answers ranging from "popcorn!" to "protein bars!"

I'm not suggesting vitaminwater did anything *wrong*. The
brand just could have achieved a lot more *by taking one extra step*.
Because once you've accumulated a million Facebook fans and
found out what snack food they like to eat with their vitaminwater, what do you do next?

Users on Facebook belong to Facebook. That means the
wealth of data they generate also belongs to Facebook. Of
course, Facebook shares *some* portion of that with the brand
itself. Facebook Insights provides brands statistics like page
views, usage numbers, and a demographic breakdown.

However, that barely scratches the surface of the analytics
that companies need to truly engage their most dedicated constituents. For all the TV ads that vitaminwater ran promoting
its Facebook page—which were the most effective? Why did
people join the site? When did they join? If the vitaminwater
team were to post a video to the brand's community page, they
could learn how many people viewed it, but not *which* people
viewed it. They therefore have no way to do future engagement
with only those people.

Let's explore just that September 4 status update: "milk &
cookies. coffee & doughnuts. vitaminwater & _____?" Unless
vitaminwater is manually recording every one of those thousand
responses, they have no way to track and log who's saying
"protein bars" and who's responding "popcorn." Drinkers of
vitaminwater are segmenting *themselves* into those who see

vitaminwater as a fitness supplement and those who view it as a snack beverage. But without a way to record that valuable information, the company can't use that demographic breakdown to further target those consumers. What if vitaminwater wants to launch a future drink with a protein supplement—or one that pairs particularly well with a Hershey bar? What if the brand launches an ad campaign targeted to gym rats and wants to get the word out? Having a simple way to message just a portion of your audience can be invaluable.

Of course, the whimsical status update probably was not intended to spark a marketing campaign—it was just meant to keep the page's users engaged. But why *shouldn't* the vitaminwater team want to track and use all the data they can? When vitaminwater has its users self-segmenting into discrete groups, shouldn't they want to be able to at least record that information? Isn't engagement without any follow-up exactly the problem?

Compare vitaminwater's missed opportunity with a promotion that *Martha Stewart Living* recently ran. Martha Stewart, as I suggested earlier in this chapter, firmly believes in catering her own party. As part of the magazine's premiere digital issue on the iPad, *Martha Stewart Living* created an exclusive video in which it asked decorators Rebecca Robertson and Kevin Sharkey each to design the same room in their preferred style. Sharkey created a more traditional-themed garden room, while Robertson used graphic lines and bright colors for a more modern look. The video then asked users to text in to vote for their favorite. Those who preferred the traditional room texted in "TRADITIONAL," and those who liked the more modern room could text in (you guessed it) "MODERN."

By using these two keywords, *Martha Stewart Living* segmented incoming responses based on people's preferred design styles. It thereby immediately gained a window into the design preferences of its users—a distinction that it could then use in the future to target just one of those groups.

That opens the door to a wealth of possibilities down the road. The company can send product offers, sponsor messages, and programming updates targeted around different design aesthetics *just* to the people who will be most interested in them. Why waste time and money trying to market a modernist Eames chair to someone who'd rather be sitting in a wingback?

To be fair, the *Martha Stewart Living* promotion is fairly simple in comparison to the massive vitaminwater campaign. There was no expensive media buy promoting it, no flavor creator apps, and no product sitting on store shelves at the end of the day. But the Martha Stewart promotion was a quick hit on a digital channel rather than the culmination of a multimillion-dollar marketing initiative. Of *course* there's a difference in scale between the two. The broader point is that when you build a mobile engagement campaign, you can see *exactly* how new members join your list, track each action they take, and ultimately follow up with messages targeted just for them. You know a lot more about your mobile subscribers than that they just "like" your product.

An integrated mobile campaign lets an organization host its own gatherings in its own digital universe, win permission for long-term communication, and create data that belongs to the company, not the social media site. That data then feeds the company's larger customer relations management, allowing it to refine its offers. Social networking is an amazing way to get your message out, but it's no substitute for ongoing, one-to-one connections. It's the difference between chatting at a party and having a relationship. Someone you meet at a party might take a passing interest if you told him or her that you prefer popcorn with your vitaminwater. He or she might even "like" that fact. But if you don't get the person's number, you have no opportunity to make an actual friend with whom you might have a long-term relationship, sharing many different bottles of vitaminwater.

Beyond just losing access to invaluable usage data, companies that sacrifice their own media for a Facebook page are often pursuing an unrealistic goal: attracting new consumers. More and more data shows that the vast majority of Facebook fans are *already* consumers of those brands. According to a recent article in *Advertising Age*, Facebook functions more as a loyalty program than a customer acquisition tool:

> Research by DDB Worldwide and Opinionway Research finds 84% of a typical brand's Facebook fans are existing customers. That makes marketing to the fan base much more like a customer relationship management program than a customer-acquisition tool for most brands, said Justin Kistner, social-media products director of web analytics from Webtrends.
>
> In fact, the DDB study shows that only 3% of a brand's Facebook fans are new consumers who haven't used the brand before, and intend to. That number is almost doubled (5%) by the percentage of Facebook fans who *have never used the brand and never plan to.*[6]

According to Sucharitu Mulpuru, a VP at consumer research giant Forrester, "On average, retailers report that only a small single-digit percent of sales can be attributed to social media"[7]—and the ROI from social media is "muddy." She elaborated to *Direct Marketing News*: "All the hype around social networks in particular lead people to think it's something they need to do."

That dismissal is definitely an overstatement. Using social media *is* something that most companies should do. At the very least, it's something they're expected to do by their consumers. Four years ago, creating a corporate MySpace page was considered a groundbreaking digital strategy. In this day and age, companies that *don't* have a Facebook page are looked at askance.

Marketers are doing the right thing—almost. They're thinking in the old broadcast way about numbers of impressions, but not making the additional stop toward actual engagement. They're hosting a giant party, but, once the guests have arrived, they're not even asking them to fill out a guest book.

As a result, they're left with vague metrics—such as number of fans or number of page views—that have no real significance beyond a marketing PowerPoint. There's nothing inherently wrong with Coke (which owns Glaceau, which makes vitaminwater) using a Facebook page to engage its existing consumers. The problem arises when strategy ends there.

And when your only metric is "attention," how do you judge that attention's quality? After Mashable reported on Denny's menu misprint snafu, a Denny's spokesperson e-mailed to argue, "We currently have more combined Twitter followers than anyone in our competitive restaurant set."[8] And even the much-maligned Chevy Tahoe campaign could point to high viewership numbers. As a CNET article about the backlash describes, the General Motors PR department actually used the campaign's viral spread to suggest its success:

> The contest is a success as a marketing campaign, according to Melisa Tezanos, a GM spokeswoman. Consumers have submitted more than 21,000 ads and have e-mailed commercials over 40,000 times, she said. Chevyapprentice.com [the campaign's website] has generated 2.4 million page views, and the average visit to the site lasts more than 9 minutes.[9]

Granted, not all of those ads were negative—the vast majority were probably in line with the campaign's goals. But there's an enormous difference between forwarding an e-mail and buying a car—and that's especially true when the e-mail that's being forwarded might be *negative* for your brand. Even if it *is* one of the positive videos that spoke well about the Chevy Tahoe, what good does it do Chevy to send out 40,000 e-mails . . . with no way of following up with either the e-mail sender or its recipient?

Social Media and Activism

Writing in the *New Yorker*, Malcolm Gladwell explores the disconnect between contemporary ideas of engagement via Facebook and classic examples of activism. He starts by describing the Woolworth's lunch counter sit-ins during the United States civil rights movement. In 1960, four African American college students sat down in the white people's section of a Woolworth's lunch counter in Greensboro, North Carolina, and refused to move—even under threat from store managers, police officers, and the Ku Klux Klan. Their protest sparked similar sit-ins across the South. Gladwell then compares the bravery and fortitude shown by the civil rights protesters with the phoned-in engagement of activism as practiced today. "Fifty years after one of the most extraordinary episodes of social upheaval in American history, we seem to have forgotten what activism is," he writes.

> Where activists were once defined by their causes, they are now defined by their tools. Facebook warriors go online to push for change. "You are the best hope for us all," James K. Glassman, a former senior State Department official, told a crowd of cyber activists. . . . Sites like Facebook, Glassman said, "give the U.S. a significant competitive advantage over terrorists. Some time ago, I said that Al Qaeda was 'eating our lunch on the Internet.' That is no longer the case. Al Qaeda is stuck in Web 1.0. The Internet is now about interactivity and conversation."
>
> These are strong, and puzzling, claims. Why does it matter who is eating whose lunch on the Internet?[10]

"Why does it matter who is eating whose lunch on the Internet?" You could ask the exact same questions about brands and their social media campaigns. We've become so dialed in to metrics about page views, unique visitors, post count, and e-mail forwards that we've lost sight of *what it's all there for*. It's an easy dichotomy to see when someone is trying to minimize the importance of al Qaeda, an organization that actually kills people, because they don't have a robust social media presence.

Gladwell goes on to suggest that Facebook activism has trivialized the definition of activism by defining it downward:

> Social networks are effective at increasing *participation*—by lessening the level of motivation that participation requires. The Facebook page of the Save Darfur Coalition has 1,282,339 members, who have donated an average of nine cents apiece. . . . A spokesperson for the Save Darfur Coalition told *Newsweek*, "We wouldn't necessarily gauge someone's value to the advocacy movement based on what they've given. This is a powerful mechanism to engage this critical population. They inform their community, attend events, volunteer. It's not something you can measure by looking at a ledger." In other words, Facebook activism succeeds not by motivating people to make a real sacrifice but by motivating them to do the things that people do when they are not motivated enough to make a real sacrifice.[11]

In the past six years, activist campaigns have proliferated that have had the same metrics of success as vitaminwater's: Facebook fans motivated, number of interactions, number of page views. For example, in 2005, the "Stop Global Warming Virtual March" debuted. To join the "march," you need to submit your name, your e-mail address, and your state. You're then automatically added to the 1,414,963 (and counting) virtual members. That number includes "marchers" who may have signed up for the campaign years ago and long since lost interest. Nevertheless, they have been "virtually marching" for six years, without even knowing it.

A "virtual march" could be a good idea if it is the spark that starts something more. Reform Immigration For America, for example, often makes first contact with new members through only the briefest virtual interaction. But as Eric Schmidt pointed out in his Dreamforce keynote speech, activism "should be judged based on outcomes"—not on attention. The challenge for an activist campaign, as with any organizational outreach, is to intermingle all media with direct engagement and use it to obtain real, demonstrable results.

Compare the "virtual march" or the Save Darfur Facebook page that Gladwell discusses with the mobile campaign by DoSomething.org. If you're not familiar with DoSomething.org, it's a youth engagement group that provides teenagers concrete steps they can take to do good in their local communities. Projects range from recycling bottles to collecting used jeans for the homeless to brainstorming new ways to reduce energy consumption. DoSomething.org is an incredible success story—and I'll be writing more about it in Chapter 8.

DoSomething.org does indeed have a Facebook page. After all—who in this world doesn't? As of this writing, the organization has over 173,000 fans, and it is featuring videos from its recent Do Something Awards. Just like vitaminwater, the organization regularly engages its fans with questions like, "Should smoking cigarettes be legal?"

What makes DoSomething.org effective is that its activism doesn't stop with Facebook: it begins there. DoSomething.org converts its Facebook members into a direct relationship. It has e-mail outreach, its awards event, and mobile outreach. Recently, it launched an SMS scavenger hunt. And of course, DoSomething .org hasn't shuttered its homepage, dosomething.org.

A Facebook page should not be the end of your activist or marketing campaign. Instead, it should only be the beginning.

Taking the Next Step

In *The Net Delusion*, the author Evgeny Morozov argues against the idea that the Internet promotes liberation and opposes tyranny. As the *New York Review of Books* describes it:

> Morozov writes that he worked to promote democracy and media reform in the former Soviet bloc by using the Internet. He and his colleagues initially believed that in "blogs, social networks, wikis" they had discovered "an arsenal of weapons . . . far more potent than police batons, surveillance cameras, and handcuffs." They were wrong, as it turned out. "Not only were our strategies failing," he recounts, "but we also noticed a significant push back from the governments."[12]

To counter the "cyber-utopianism" that suggests that Twitter is an unmitigated force for societal good, Morozov describes a litany of ways that the Internet has further empowered repressive regimes. In Iran, the government uses digital media to further surveil its citizens. In China and Russia, the state funds progovernment bloggers who promote the party line. Venezuela's Hugo Chávez has a Twitter account with over 2 million followers.

The lesson is that digital media by themselves don't actually accomplish anything. The more important issue is who is using the media and what they are trying to do with them.

The question of digital media's role in activism was raised again recently, after the Egyptian revolution of February 2011. Numerous cyber-utopianists started proclaiming that the world was witnessing the first-ever Facebook revolution. CNN dubbed it "Revolution 2.0."[13] According to this narrative, the protests across Tunisia, Egypt, and Libya had been created on Facebook. They'd been nurtured on Facebook. And nobody in Egypt would even have been able to *find* Tahrir Square without Mark Zuckerberg personally giving them directions.

That narrative was nurtured by some within Egypt, too. "I want to meet Mark Zuckerberg one day and thank him," said Wael Ghonim, one of the primary digital activists who operated within Egypt. "This revolution started online. This revolution started on Facebook. . . . I always said that if you want to liberate a society, just give them the Internet."[14]

But much of the Egyptian protestors' infrastructure existed well before anybody decided to make a Facebook page. There were the remains of previous youth groups that had been splintered by government repression. There were disaffected bloggers. There was the Academy for Change, a group of Egyptian expatriates who had been living in Qatar.[15]

But the activists in Egypt *did* use Facebook and other technologies to help them build scale fast. They were able to communicate with a vast number of people much more quickly by building a sympathetic online community. As the *New York Review of Books* describes it, "Facebook groups interacted online with others of like mind, and also with traditional protest organizers, such as trade unions and political parties."

While Facebook groups helped the protesters build scale, much of the core planning and organizing was done through classic person-to-person communication. Small groups of people texted each other information and logistics. Facebook was being monitored by the government—and anyway, text messages were more immediate and more personal.

The Egyptian protesters used social media *correctly*. They built an audience on Facebook, and then translated it into direct person-to-person communication. They sparked their movement on Facebook and then turned to text messages to make that movement personal and inspire concrete action.

The challenge for any organization, from a revolution to a consumer brand, is—how do you spread your message broadly enough to reach the most supporters, and also keep it personal enough to move them to action? How do you preach to the largest audience and still inspire every person?

Throughout this chapter, I've been talking about how organizations that use Facebook are often missing that "next step." The Egyptian protest showed one way to take that step. And Martha Stewart came up with another.

As we've discussed in the Introduction, Martha Stewart built her mobile list for her Dinner Tonight campaign by offering a daily dinner recipe. Those people who were interested in that recipe could text back the word "COOK" to receive a shopping list, an e-mail of the full recipe, and a text message coupon for one of the ingredients.

The Dinner Tonight campaign gave general information to a wide audience—and offered specific action steps and offers for those who wanted to learn more. And as discussed in the Introduction, Martha Stewart found that each day, more than 20 percent of the users asked for the day's recipe—and it was a different 20 percent every time.

Cooking dinner is a little less intense than turning out to protest the government. And creating one centralized mobile list might have been outside the scope of the grassroots movement in Tahrir Square. But imagine that the Egyptian protest movement *was* able to create a centralized list of its participants and create a campaign modeled on Martha Stewart Dinner Tonight. Organizers could send their list a brief update with every planned activity. Those members who were interested in learning more could text back, and receive more complete instructions on organizational logistics and planning.

By using what people tell you, the wealth of freely provided data that users provide, and analytics, a mobile marketing campaign can bridge scale and personalization.

One of the problems with social media activism that Gladwell cites is that network-based campaigns have no built-in hierarchy. The civil rights movement, he writes, was incredibly well-run through a rigid top-down organization. On the other hand, "Social media are not about this kind of hierarchical organization. Facebook and the like are tools for building *networks*, which are the opposite, in structure and character, of hierarchies."

The power of a mobile campaign is that it can provide you the reach of a network with the top-down structure of a traditional hierarchy.

Of course, Martha Stewart doesn't always have *all* the answers. The Dinner Tonight campaign could also learn a lot from the Egyptian protesters. The way in which the protesters *combined* media magnified their impact. The protesters mixed Facebook pages with text messages and Skype calls. And of course, they used the ultimate medium, which was widespread grassroots action—the actual protests themselves.

Any effective movement needs to combine broad reach with the personal and local. It needs to appeal to the country and to the neighborhood. And it needs to take into account actual results. Social media are a powerful tool. But they are just a tool, only as good as the results-oriented strategy that employs them. Targeted, segmented messaging, particularly mobile messaging, can help you take the next step from broadcast media to actual one-to-one engagement.

In the following chapters, we'll explain the step-by-step process of how to start a mobile campaign and achieve that truly personal connection.

STEP 1:
MAKE THE
ONE-TO-ONE
CONNECTION

The Baltimore Aquarium wanted to woo tourists, a group likely to have the time and the inclination to visit. But how to reach them? Tourists, only in town for a short time, were not likely to watch much local television, listen to local radio, or otherwise make themselves available to an advertiser in traditional ways. They might see ads in Baltimore's airports and train stations, or on highway billboards and tourist information handouts, but even if they saw those ads, at such hectic moments how much information could they retain and use? A driver in an unfamiliar city, or even a plane traveler picking up luggage, was probably not going to have the free attention to take in details—or the free hand to make notes even when a message got through. Baltimore Aquarium's marketers knew whom they wanted to reach, but not how to reach them effectively. How could they outfox the disconnect?

The aquarium's marketers realized that not one but four steps were necessary to reach, understand, inspire, and retain the people on whom their success depended:

1. **Make the one-to-one connection.** Where could they find tourists who were excited to learn what they could do in a new city, with enough free attention to learn about the aquarium's new exhibits and shows? One innovative idea: they were arriving on airplanes. Baltimore Aquarium arranged a tie-in with Jet Blue in which the airline offered information as the plane taxied to the gate. Here was a captive audience, fresh to the city, with some free attention (it's boring waiting for permission to disembark), just waiting to see something new.

2. **Discover the one-to-one opportunities.** The goal of this campaign was not just the traditional advertising approach of exposing a captive audience to a commercial message; it was also to find an opportunity for mutual benefit by offering content that was relevant and compelling to this specific audience at this moment. Right after a Jet Blue plane touched down in Baltimore, just as travelers were being welcomed to the city by the flight attendant and probably wondering what to do there, they were offered a relevant answer.

3. **Inspire action.** The commercial didn't just convey information, it asked travelers to donate to the aquarium. As passengers turned their cell phones back on, the advertisement invited them to text in a small donation to support the aquarium's goals. It was easy: there was nothing to remember, nothing to write

down, and nothing else they had to be doing at that moment. All they had to do in response was to use the device that was already powering up in their hands. By reminding passengers of the importance of the aquarium's mission, the advertisement spurred interest in the Baltimore Aquarium even in those travelers who chose not to donate.

4. **Develop a long-term relationship.** Once passengers donated to the aquarium by sending a text, they opened the door for continued engagement. In addition to its text to donate initiative, the Baltimore Aquarium runs a mobile campaign that features quizzes, contests, discounts on merchandise, and messages encouraging people to visit the website. The aquarium could turn passing interest into a visit and, in time, even membership. And it could track the developing relationship with each person who's a member of its mobile list.

This chapter describes the overall process of translating a company's situation, goals, and available media technologies into making first contact with your target audience: making the **one-to-one connection**. Rather than necessarily building a campaign from scratch, *use what you have* by pairing mobile with your organization's existing approaches. Stonyfield Farm put its text-in campaign on the tops of its yogurt cups; Reform Immigration For America put it on the handmade signs that protestors held up during rallies. If you load a *Wikipedia* page on your phone, there's a space at the top of the page asking you to text in to make a donation. The goal is not to *replace* an organization's existing media plan but to *pair it strategically* with mobile.

Then, in the next three chapters, we'll explore campaigns built with each of the three other steps as their centerpieces, emphasizing how each one helps take integrated mobile campaigns beyond traditional advertising and marketing, with case studies drawn from private-sector, nonprofit, and public-sector examples.

One-to-One for Everyone

"Using the existing media you have" doesn't have to be as elaborate as surprising people on an airplane or printing a text call to action on your yogurt lids. For many organizations, building the one-to-one connection can start with simply putting a mobile call to action in your existing media outreach. Whatever television ads or print materials you're using to drive people to your website can simply be repurposed to ask people to text in to a short code. By adding in a text call to action, you increase your response rates and open the door for further engagement.

For example, the National Coalition for Safer Roads ran a public service announcement (PSA) in support of red light cameras in Missouri. At the end of the PSA, which highlights the true stories of people whose lives have been affected by red light runners, viewers are asked to "text RED to 723389" to learn more (see Figure 3.1). Similarly, the Iraq and Afghanistan Veterans of America (IAVA) used billboard advertisements to

Figure 3.1   **Calls to action can be incorporated into any of your existing media—from a print ad to a public service announcement to a yogurt lid.** (*Photos by National Coalition for Safer Roads, Worthy Publishing, and Harriet Rosin.*)

ask veterans to text in "VETS' to 69866. When VH1 and Do Something wanted to engage people around their Save the Music campaign, they asked them to text in "BATTLE" to 30644 for more information. These organizations took materials they already had—a PSA or a poster—and simply added in instructions for people to text.

Most people have their cell phones with them at all times, whether they're walking down the street or watching television. It's considerably easier for them to text in a keyword than to get up, go to their computer, and log on to your website. Putting a mobile call to action in an existing ad translates a spark of interest that these ads create into an actual connection. That may seem intuitive, but marketers for Chicago's Shedd Aquarium put that theory to the test in June 2009, when they were promoting the aquarium's new aquatic show, Fantasea. One flight of their television ads asked people to log on to a website to learn more and enter a contest for free VIP tickets. Another set of ads asked users to text in the word "FOX" (the network the ads aired on) to a short code. The television ad with the SMS call to action generated 325 percent more contest entries than the web call to action.

Using social media is another great way to drive mobile engagement. We wrote in the last chapter that social media provide a superb tool for building an audience—but not such a superb tool for generating sales or gathering extensive user data. Many of our clients ask their Facebook fans to join their mobile list, or tweet a call to action to their Twitter followers. Facebook and Twitter fans are already engaged with your organization. They've taken the initiative to hit "like" or "follow." They're primed to take the next step and engage with you over their phones.

Asking passersby, casual television viewers, or Facebook surfers to text in is a simple way to begin a conversation. Right away, you know they're interested parties, and you have their phone numbers. That's already some of the most valuable information you can gather. Organizations can then immediately follow up to ask for further information, such as respondents' name or e-mail address, or what their interests are. The National Coalition for Safer Roads asked new members to text in with the most dangerous intersections they knew. The NCSR could then take that information and start to compile a database of where video cameras could be most effective. These messages also made new members feel that they were already having a concrete impact in the fight for safer roads.

After that initial first contact, you can choose to either keep new members siloed or slowly integrate them into your broader outreach. Some organizations target *just* their newest members with "welcome series" messaging—messages scheduled based on the date the subscribers joined the campaign. That way, you can introduce new members to your goals slowly and engage them with your values before you send them a fund-raising message or a coupon down the road.

One-to-One for Events

Using your existing advertising campaign to support a mobile call to action is probably the most basic way of going one-to-one. In general, organizations should use the assets they have to promote their mobile list and start a conversation that can lead to lifelong engagement. Groups that throw events, for example, or have access to large venues often have a huge captive audience—but an audience that's going to leave the venue in a couple of hours. Putting a mobile call to action in a prominent place can turn a one-time contact into an ongoing engaged membership.

The Sacramento Kings and the ARCO Arena (now the Power Balance Pavilion) where the Kings play had an extremely successful mobile campaign. They used the power of their sporting events and captive audience to build a one-to-one relationship with sports fans and event-goers.

The Kings could assume that a person who attended one Kings game would probably be interested in attending another. The people who are showing up to their games are definitely sports fans, likely Kings fans, and there's a good chance they live in or near Sacramento. Therefore, at events and games throughout the year, the arena broadcasts its mobile call to action. The Kings told sports fans to text in and join its mobile list to be the first to hear scores and breaking news about the game. At some events, it asked attendees to text in to report if something was wrong with their seat. It also gave access to special offers and contests—for example, asking its fans to text in for an exclusive invitation to a player appearance. The Kings used the assets it has—an arena of dedicated fans, access to player appearances, and the inside scoop on breaking Kings news—to compile a list of engaged fans eager to hear from the Kings on a regular basis. The Kings then used that list not only to keep its fans engaged with scores and breaking news, but also to send out ticket offers and merchandise deals.

At one game, the Kings asked fans to text in to its mobile list to get 15 percent off tickets to the next week's game. It sent an auto-reply to fans who texted in, which the fans could show to dedicated agents at the arena to receive the ticket discount. The Kings guessed that around 5 percent of the game's attendees texted in for the coupon code. Not only did the promotion build its mobile list, it had a direct impact on ticket sales.

In addition just targeting Kings fans, the ARCO Arena used a separate mobile list to target those interested in going to large-scale events. Just as there's a good chance that a fan at a Kings game will be interested in going to another Kings game—so too it's a good bet that an attendee at a large event in Sacramento will be interested in attending other types of events in the future. The arena therefore used a separate short code for those who wanted to get advance notice of, say, when Britney Spears was coming to town next. ARCO found that a text message blast to the Arena list generated $10 to $12 in incremental sales for *every name on that list*. That means that for a 1,000-person list, a text blast would generate $10,000 to $12,000. Additionally, ARCO offered the same promotion over Facebook and Twitter—and found that its mobile list had a significantly greater increase to sales than did social media.

The Kings' and ARCO's text message campaigns actually demonstrate all four steps of building a one-to-one relationship. The campaigns used the captive audience in the Arco arena to **(1) make a one-to-one relationship**. They then **(2) discovered the one-to-one opportunities** by realizing that a fan at one

Kings game would probably be interested in another and that a Sacramento event-goer might be interested in more than just basketball. They **(3) inspired action** by offering player appearances and ticket discounts to spur people to join the list. And they **(4) developed a long-term relationship** by continuing that engagement past the one-off merchandise opportunities through ongoing promotions and sending updated scores and breaking news. But building that engaged mobile list started with simply taking advantage of the assets the organization already had.

Teen heartthrobs the Jonas Brothers made the one-to-one connection with their fans in a similar fashion. The Jonas Brothers became involved in DoSomething.org—an organization mentioned previously in the book, but that deserves endless accolades for its groundbreaking work in engaging young people over mobile. With teenagers hanging on their every adorable word, the Jonas Brothers wanted to get the Do Something message out in such a way that it would have the broadest possible impact.

The Jonas Brothers chose to spark that one-to-one connection when they performed a concert at President Obama's inaugural. The concert was broadcast on VH1 and across the Internet—and Joe, Nick, and Kevin took a moment to speak to their live and at-home audiences, passing the mike from one to another brother:

> We have set up a special way for fans to volunteer in their
> own home towns. You just have to text "JONAS" to 30644
> and you will get a welcome message asking for your zip

code. Once you do that, you'll start getting the names of non-profit organizations that you can use to help in your community. You want to make a difference? Text us and start volunteering.

It was difficult to hear the Jonas Brothers over the screaming teenage fans. Nevertheless, as a result of this single call to action, thousands of people texted in to join the DoSomething.org campaign.

The Sacramento Kings have a giant arena that can fit thousands of sports fans and concertgoers. The Jonas Brothers have a passionate audience of screaming teenagers. But your organization doesn't need a sports arena or a pop supergroup to build a one-to-one connection with a captive audience.

St. Jude Children's Research Hospital is an inspiring organization dedicated to helping young children with cancer and other terminal illnesses. It has moved thousands of college leaders around the country to get involved as fund-raisers and campus activists. At its annual Collegiate Leadership Seminar, it gathers around 600 of the most dedicated leaders, who are in charge of coordinating fund-raising at their schools to create awareness and raise money for St. Jude. The college leaders come from two primary groups—Tri Delta Fraternity members and the St. Jude's Up 'til Dawn program, where teams raise money to compete in an all-night challenge at their campuses. The Collegiate Leadership Seminar hosts these college leaders in Memphis for a three-day seminar full of presentations about how to better coordinate events on their campuses.

What St. Jude's marketers realized was that, with their collegiate leaders, they had an excellent opportunity to build a mobile list of their most engaged young supporters. Every single person at the conference had a mobile phone, and in between sessions or on breaks, they had nothing to do. With 600 people just waiting for the next presentation, and with screens throughout the conference room, St. Jude's team thought that this might be the perfect opportunity for a mobile call to action.

St. Jude created its one-to-one connection by asking engaging multiple-choice questions on the screens, to which the conference-goers could text in responses. "How hot is Memphis?" was one of the questions—to which a sample reply was, "I want to jump in the Mississippi River." (The event took place in the summer.) It also offered attendees a text-to-win promotion, asking them to text in "CLS" to win an iTunes gift card or St. Jude T-shirt.

St. Jude's results showed that it didn't matter what the gift was that it was offering—the captive and engaged attendees were willing to text in to be a part of the promotion. Over 30 percent of the audience texted in, and every opt-in provided the responder's name and e-mail as a follow-up.

As part of its mobile outreach St. Jude also printed a QR code on the conference schedules and on the conference directional materials. QR codes (see Figure 3.2) are black-and-white square graphics similar to bar codes that can be placed on any type of printed material, whether it's a flier, a bus advertisement, or a point of sale standee. Using any one of numerous free scanning apps, people can scan the code and be immediately taken to your mobile website or other digital material.

Figure 3.2 **A sample QR code.**

St. Jude's QR codes gave readers access to a digital copy of the schedule—and gave St. Jude further information about the event attendees. Even though St. Jude's marketers forgot to print instructions on the schedules about *how* to scan the QR codes, they still found that almost 28 percent of the attendees scanned the codes.

Since its College Leadership Seminar event, St. Jude has continued to engage the youth activists who joined its mobile list. Every month, it sends out a mass text to the entire list with the story of a "patient of the month," providing the history, diagnosis, and interests of one of St. Jude's patients. The heartrending yet inspiring stories are intended to keep St. Jude's most dedicated members engaged and attuned to the vital importance of the St. Jude mission. Attached to that message, St. Jude usually includes a link to a video of the patient so that those with Internet access can view the video on their device as well.

Moreover, because of the power of mobile to segment messaging, St. Jude can specifically target *just* the college leaders without speaking to the entire mobile list. The CLS attendees are segregated by opt-in keywords, so St. Jude can reach out to just them. Because the leadership training seminar happened over the summer, St. Jude's marketers wanted to make sure that the college students were engaged at the Up 'til Dawn events in the fall. Therefore, once the events start launching at their respective schools, St. Jude sends out inspiring reminders. The messages remind the list members to keep fund-raising—and also to forward on the text messages to their friends.

The hundreds of college leaders that St. Jude reached may not have had the scope of the thousands of responses that the Jonas Brothers inspired, or the tens of thousands of arena-goers at Sacramento's ARCO Arena. But by selectively targeting the college leaders and then fostering that relationship through sustained engagement, St. Jude was able to build one-to-one relationships with its most dedicated supporters.

When One-to-One Goes Viral

One of the smartest things St. Jude did throughout its mobile campaign was to ask its college leadership members to forward on its messages. Sometimes the best way to get the word out about your organization is to have other people spread the word for you. The organizations featured throughout this chapter had their existing assets work for them when they built their one-to-one connections. Those assets can be an ad campaign, a giant sports arena, a yogurt top, or a website. But those assets can also be the people who care the most about you.

It's unlikely that anyone is going to get extremely passionate about promoting his or her favorite soft drink. But some causes, like St. Jude's, do inspire that kind of fanatical devotion that leads people to *want* to make the one-to-one introduction between an organization and their peers.

As mentioned earlier in this chapter, Reform Immigration For America spreads the word about its mobile list by having its members include the text call to action on the signs they carry at protests. Protests are a great way to find thousands and thousands of passionate people who are uniquely focused at that moment on promoting your organization's message. They also will typically have their phone on them. Transforming a call to action from an organizational mandate to a moment of communal engagement built out RI4A's grassroots infrastructure.

It's not only social causes that inspire that kind of devotion. College sports teams are another group with passionate fans who are willing to do anything for their team. For the past 10 years, Capital One Bank has hosted a Mascot Challenge to "find the nation's best mascot." In 2010, for example, Old Dominion's Big Blue beat out Louisiana State University's Mike the Tiger and UCLA's Joe Bruin, among others, for ultimate bragging rights.

The winner is determined by fan votes, and users text to vote for their favorite mascot. In support of their mascots, fans and schools make and circulate videos across the web with the call to action to support their team, and they take the competition to social media. "Brutus! Brutus! Brutus! Text "BRUTUS" to 69866 to vote our No. 1 Nut to the top in Capital One Mascot Challenge!" tweeted one Ohio State Buckeyes fan, who attached a training montage of Brutus Buckeye. Over 5 million votes later, Capital One Bank had a mobile database of engaged college fans who it knew were passionate about their schools and passionate about sports.

One-to-One in Media

Media organizations today face an increasing challenge. New forms of digital communication have fractured their audience and taken a significant bite into their advertising revenues. The second quarter of 2011 marked a "depressing milestone" for newspapers, according to Yahoo News. "Newspapers brought in nearly $6 billion from print and online advertising combined during the second quarter, a 7 percent decline from the same time in 2010." That makes April–June the fifth consecutive year of consistent ad revenue decline.[1]

"Old media" like newspapers and radio are looking for new ways to engage their traditional audiences. Groups like WNYC and the *New York Times* are brainstorming innovative ways to keep their members informed and establish a beachhead in the new media era by building out interactive elements to their reportage. Their mobile campaigns can range from sending tune-in alerts for new shows to asking citizen journalists to text in local updates during a natural disaster.

For those who work in media, making the one-to-one connection can be fairly straightforward. Media groups already have an existing way to reach their audience. The *New York Times* can run an ad in its newspaper. Martha Stewart can turn an iPad video into a text call to action. WNYC can make a call to action on the air.

For example, on Christmas of 2010, a massive snowstorm left New Yorkers stranded in a sea of white. The blizzard grounded flights and clogged city streets. City transit was all but shut down, and many New Yorkers were unable to leave their homes.

As a service to city residents—and a testament to the city's slow response—WNYC asked users to text in whether or not their streets had been plowed. It used its airwaves to tell listeners to text in "PLOW" to its mobile short code, and it made a similar call to action on its website. WNYC then geolocated where the texts were originating and plotted that information on a Google map. (See Figure 3.3 for an example of one day's map.) White balloons represent unplowed streets; dark balloons represent plowed streets.

The daily maps tracked the city's progress in digging out from under the snowstorm. And they gave a voice to frustrated city residents, who included texted comments and downloadable voice mails. "Elderly and disabled need [a] pathway," wrote one. "There's cars abandoned and stuck in the snow all over the

Figure 3.3 **WNYC's Google map showed plowed and unplowed streets.**

place," another noted in a voice mail. ("Still stuck here on the beach in sunny Puerto Rico," a traveler gloated.) The maps gave the lie to New York City Mayor Michael Bloomberg's claim that the city had the street cleanup under control. They provided visual proof that residents were trapped in unplowed streets—particularly in the city's outer boroughs.

WNYC's programming also used click-to-call technology. People had the option to leave voice mails for WNYC, which the radio station was then able to play on the air, providing first-person anecdotes from people they normally would never hear from. "We had at least 50 or 60 voice mails of people telling their stories that we could play on-air," WNYC's digital editor Jim Colgan said. "You think of what reporters are doing—going out and getting stories wherever they can go. We could extend the reach of the voices we had on the air."

In addition to driving programming and creating a valuable information resource, the "plow map" gave WNYC a database of concerned citizens it could then reach out to again and again. Initially, the station simply asked for follow-up on the developing conditions of the street cleanup. Shortly afterward, it asked about trash collection. And moving forward, WNYC is able to ask its citizen-journalists for on-the-block feedback to any number of questions.

WNYC's plow map is a great example of a media organization using its built-in infrastructure to create a one-to-one connection with a wide audience across the city. As Jim Colgan said, these were citizens that WNYC's reporters normally would not be able to reach. Through its mobile campaign, WNYC was able to engage listeners in new ways and drive its programming.

The campaign is another great example of all four steps of a mobile campaign. WNYC **made the one-to-one relationship** with calls to action on its website and over its airwaves. It **discovered the one-to-one opportunities** when it realized that it had an enraged audience eager to speak out about the conditions in their neighborhoods. It **inspired action** when it gave this audience the chance to be heard—through the map and on the air—merely by texting in. And it **developed a long-term relationship** by continuing to ask its mobile users for updates about city services in their neighborhoods.

For some media organizations, however, making the one-to-one connection doesn't always mean just a mass blast across all their existing outlets. The power of mobile is that it can be targeted precisely—and sometimes even a media outlet with a passionate audience of millions needs to get creative in building the perfect one-to-one connection.

This American Life is one of the most popular shows on public radio. The weekly mix of "essays, memoirs, field recordings, short fiction, and found footage"[2] goes out to about 1.7 million listeners on over 500 stations. Hundreds of thousands more download the show's podcast.

Unlike network media, however, public media are not supported by advertising. Public radio is entirely reliant on donations for its funding. And many radio programs like *This American Life* have a problem: the radio stations themselves don't want their programs soliciting donations on-air.

The reason is that radio stations have semiannual fund-raising drives of their own. They believe that when the radio shows themselves solicit for donations, it takes away from the station's fund-raising initiatives. If listeners are donating just to their favorite shows, they may not find it worthwhile to give to the stations that air them.

For *This American Life*, making the one-to-one connection meant taking stock of the show's assets and realizing that the show's marketers could create a specific, targeted fund-raising request to just their *podcast* listeners. Because the podcast is downloaded online, it's not playing over the radio waves. So *This American Life*'s host Ira Glass could insert a request just in the podcast, and no feathers would be ruffled at the show's radio affiliates.

And what better way to reach podcast listeners than to ask for a mobile text-to-give donation? Most people who listen to podcasts download them onto their mobile phones and listen on the go. Asking those listeners to go to a website and donate would be ineffective. By the time they reached a computer, they probably would already have forgotten all about the donation request. But because podcast listeners already have their phones in their hands, it's a simple, top-of-mind activity for them to text in a donation. As Seth Lind, the show's production manager, told the website Mobile Active:

> Our traditional way of asking for donations on a podcast was sending people to a website—if you're out jogging, you're not really going to do that. But if you're out jogging listening to the show on your iPhone or another smartphone that plays media, maybe you would stop and take the 30 seconds or less to send a text. We thought that it could lower the bar for people and make it a lot easier to donate.[3]

That's exactly what happened. A few times a year, Ira Glass comes on the air and says, for example, "I'm asking you to pitch in. Basically, cover our cost to get the show to you. . . . Text "TAL" to the phone number 25383, and when you do that, 10 bucks goes to us. A 10-dollar donation will appear on your phone bill." And Lind was absolutely right. By the time of the Mobile Active article in 2010, *This American Life* had made the one-to-one connection with tens of thousands of new donors.

These are just a few of the thousands of innovative companies that are building the one-to-one connection. They're taking advantage of the media they have and their existing assets to reach consumers and build a mobile list. But building the connection is just the first step. In the next chapter, you'll see how you can take the data from your mobile list to discover the one-to-one opportunities that can truly transform your organizational outreach.

STEP 2:

DISCOVER THE

ONE-TO-ONE

OPPORTUNITIES

Imagine a man and a woman at a party, two strangers "across a crowded room." He catches her eye, and something almost magical starts to happen. Drawn together, they feel they must speak. As if by agreement, they move toward each other through the crowd. They leave pleasantries behind.

The man says, "I have a feeling about you."

The woman says, "I know what you mean—it's as if we've known each other longer than just tonight."

Then the man gazes into her eyes and says, "I know we've only just met, but I want to give you something." He reaches into his pocket and pulls out a small card. "Here," he says. "This coupon gets ladies half-price drinks on Tuesdays."

Too often, companies make connections with the audience they need to reach, winning permission to communicate privately with them and beginning to establish a relationship of mutual interest and trust—and then squander that connection on trivial marketing ploys. The opportunity in any interaction in the digital age is to gather data and learn everything you can about potential customers in order to discover all the opportunities for mutual benefit. A mobile connection can lead to so much more than a mass-produced offer with no regard for its recipient.

Throughout the last chapter, examples of organizations finding the one-to-one opportunities are largely cases of intuition. The Sacramento Kings realized that people attending its games were definitely basketball fans, probably Kings fans, and most likely lived in Sacramento. The Baltimore Aquarium had the insight that tourists waiting to disembark from Jet Blue flights would be a perfect captive audience.

But the revolutionary potential of a mobile campaign is that you don't need savvy guesswork to find the best opportunities to reach your audience. You can rely on mobile data. In this chapter, we'll look at the sources of data available through an integrated mobile campaign. We'll also explore real-world examples of how our customers have used that data to create opportunities that reach their users in a way that's meaningful to them. We'll contrast the mobile approach to Google's AdSense advertising and show that while Google does a good job targeting specific users with messages tailored to their online interests, a mobile campaign can be an even more effective marketing tool because your audience has given you long-term permission to collect their data, tailor your messages, and then send those messages in ways that won't get lost. Our unique approach here is drawn from our experience with nonprofits, which have a lot to teach the for-profit world. Nonprofits have no choice but to do extraordinary marketing: they raise money from people and give nothing to that person in return. This means they have a huge incentive to understand who is likely to care strongly about the mission of the organization.

How Getting It Wrong Can Teach You to Get It Right

To illustrate how data can shape your understanding of your target audience, consider this story about one of Mobile Commons' biggest mistakes.

As previously mentioned, the Reform Immigration For America (RI4A) campaign maintains two separate lists—one for English speakers and another for Spanish speakers (see Chapter 1). Because its rallying cry of immigration reform inspires large numbers of speakers of both languages, it sends its outreach separately to both lists.

In advance of a big meeting with the White House, RI4A wanted to give its dedicated members a chance to get involved in the debate. So it texted out a message asking its members to send in *their* questions—with the promise that the top questions would be asked at the meeting. The text read:

> Immigration Alert: BIG White House meeting w/ pro-immigrant advocates tomorrow. Text your question now. Top Qs will be asked! Txt STOP to unsub Please Forward

That unsubscribe language at the end is fairly standard opt-out language. To ensure that nobody receives text message spam, the carriers legally require that you regularly remind your audience how to unsubscribe from your mobile list. While spending valuable characters in a 160-character message can be frustrating for marketers, it sends a signal to your audience that nobody should be getting a text message who doesn't want it.

After the broadcast went out, thousands of people texted in their questions for the meeting. But we were shocked to see that the message also triggered a tidal wave of opt-outs. RI4A received 2,246 opt-out requests—five times more than any other message and about a fifth of the total unsubscribes the campaign *ever* received.

At first, our heads were spinning as RI4A's inbox was swamped with unsubscribes. Marketers in any medium know how hard-fought a battle it can be to gain each and every new subscriber. To lose over 2,000 members in just a few moments seemed like a catastrophe.

But when we started to analyze the data, we quickly realized that the vast majority of these opt-outs were coming from the Spanish-language list. Of course, there didn't seem to be anything particularly offensive about asking RI4A's Spanish-language users to text in their questions. Working backward, we realized that we had a problem of translation.

When RI4A had translated "Txt STOP to unsub" into Spanish, the translator used the word "ALTO"—a word that has special significance in the Spanish-speaking immigration reform community. "ALTO" is the rallying cry to STOP the raids—to STOP the deportation of innocent people. Many of the users who texted back "ALTO" were trying to send a message to Homeland Security Secretary Janet Napolitano, not quit the RI4A mobile list. We had to dig through the accidental unsubscribes and figure out a way to reengage them.

That mistake taught us a lot. On a practical level, we decided that from then on, anytime that anybody unsubscribed, we would send a message confirming the person had been unsubscribed from the list and telling the recipient to reply "oops" if it had been a mistake. That way, an errant "STOP" would no longer opt out an engaged user.

The broader lesson of that mistake is that different groups respond differently to different kinds of messaging. It's vitally important to engage your audience with precisely the message that means the most to them. But it can be difficult to guess how certain groups will respond to certain appeals. That's why data can be so invaluable to your campaign—because it provides concrete evidence of what issues a user cares about and how he or she wants to be reached.

In this case, the mobile data taught us how we got it wrong. The point of this chapter is to show how mobile data can help you get it *right*. Most of the examples show organizations using information to refine their messaging and better connect with their users. The RI4A mistake taught us what they were *not* responding to—or, really, what they were responding to *negatively*—and thereby allowed us to better target that audience in the future.

Since that mistake, RI4A has tested to find the best way to include an opt-out message—how to structure a message so that it spurs action, but only the action you *want*. In its next call to action—encouraging President Obama to come down hard on Arizona's racial profiling law—RI4A sent out multiple varieties of opt-out language, each to a different segment of its list. Then, for each message that it sent, it compared the unsubscribe rates and the action rates to see which messages had the biggest *positive* impact and the smallest *negative* impact. For English language messages, it found that it's fine to include an opt-out option within the body of a text. But for Spanish-language users, because of the structure of the Spanish language, it's better to send an occasional stand-alone message.

Knowing your audience can mean the difference between engaging a passionate supporter and driving away a curious participant. The power of a mobile campaign is that you can learn an incredible amount about your audience—not just the issues they care about, but even the words they react to.

The Types of Mobile Data

We've mentioned a few times throughout this book the importance of keeping track of *every* piece of data that your users generate. In this section, we will explain exactly what that means and how our customers use that information to better engage their users. Of course, we can't individually run through *every* piece of data when there is literally an infinity of different kinds of things you can track. But we will discuss some of the most basic types of data that Mobile Commons gathers and how even that baseline can help an organization find the one-to-one opportunities with its users.

First and foremost, as soon as someone texts in to your mobile campaign, you can record his or her phone number. That may sound obvious, but when you think about it, it's an incredibly powerful piece of information. If a person visits a restaurant or stops by an art gallery, the institution has that person's patronage for one visit, but it has no way to encourage him or her to come back. The gallery can't inform the patron about a new exhibition; the restaurant can't let him or her know about new specials on the menu or a discount for returning customers. The institution has to rely on the customer choosing to come in again—or, at best, choosing to visit its website.

On the other hand, for *every person who texts in to join your list*, you have a *concrete way of reaching him or her again with more information*. That immediately sets a mobile campaign apart from other types of user engagement. That's true even of digital engagement. As mentioned in Chapter 2, many forms of digital engagement track aggregate usage statistics, but they don't always correlate them to individual users.

Along with phone numbers, a mobile campaign tracks the way that new users join your list. A mobile call to action typically asks someone to text a keyword to a short code—a 5- or 6-digit phone number). Your mobile campaign can keep track of which users texted in which keyword. I've already mentioned how the ASPCA uses that information to segment dog lovers from cat lovers and RI4A distinguishes English speakers from Spanish speakers.

Segmenting by keyword also lets you see which of your appeals are the most effective. You can have a bus call to action that asks people to text in "BUS" and a radio call to action that tells them to text in "RADIO." You can then immediately see which of those advertisements is reaching more people. Alternatively, you could try out two different sets of advertising creative—each with a different keyword. One set of creative could tell users to text in "AD1," and the other creative could tell users to text in "AD2." You then could compare which of the two campaigns was more effective.

Your ability to measure the effectiveness of your advertising doesn't stop with just seeing how many people join using each keyword. You can also compare that data against the actions those people take later on. A mobile campaign can keep track of *every single action* your users take through your mobile campaign. That includes any further text messages they send, whether or not they donate, if they call Congress on your behalf, how long they stay on the phone, or if they redeem a coupon. If you send out a link to a mobile web page, you can automatically generate a unique link for every user so that you can track specifically which users are taking which actions on your mobile website (see Figure 4.1).

So, in the case of the two advertising campaigns, mobile data will not only let you know which set of advertising caused

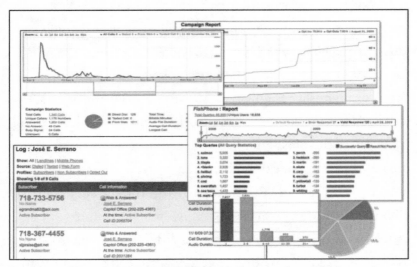

Figure 4.1   **A sampling of the variety of reports that can take mobile data and analyze user activity.** (*The Mobile Commons platform.*)

more people to join your mobile list. You *also* can tell which set of advertising was more likely to lead to a sale or to a donation. Because as nice as it is to have a huge mobile list, campaigns need to remain focused on what that list is meant to accomplish—whether that's driving advocacy, spurring donations, or increasing sales. To quote Google's Eric Schmidt once again, a campaign should not be judged on how many people are "heard"—it "should be judged based on outcomes."[1]

If that sounds confusing, picture it this way. Let's say you're an advocacy group that's campaigning against a new tax on ice cream. You run two ads—one that says, "Stop the tax on ice cream," and another that just shows a picture of a delicious ice cream cone. More people might text in for the delicious ice cream cone, but those people might not be the staunchest advocates in the long political battle for ice cream tax reform. With a mobile campaign, you'll be able to determine that the "Stop the tax on ice cream" advertisement actually had a more substantial benefit to your organization.

After people join your mobile campaign, it's standard practice to ask them for a little more information about themselves. The next set of information is typically their name, their e-mail address, and their postal address or zip code. Some organizations ask for age and gender. We've seen upward of 90 percent response rates when companies ask mobile users for follow-up information.

A zip code is a powerful tool for outreach. Suddenly, your national list of mobile subscribers becomes an opportunity for local engagement. You can message people based on where they live and connect them with opportunities near them. People connect much more naturally with local events that are happening down the block than with campaigns happening a thousand miles away (see Figure 4.2).

A number of organizations are already doing this kind of local outreach. One of the most effective is Organizing for America (OFA), the Obama campaign. With an enormous database of supporters across the country, the Obama campaign's nationwide reach is unparalleled. But in order to create a national movement, the campaign needs to inspire local action.

Organizing for America's outreach is not just focused on getting Obama reelected. It also tries to have an impact on winning the local elections that are vital for Obama to get his legislative agenda through Congress. In 2011, Democrats faced

Figure 4.2   **A text message "conversation" allows you to ask your users for a wide range of information.** [*A Mobile Commons campaign as seen on an iPhone.*]

special elections in Los Angeles, New York, and Wisconsin. OFA wanted to mobilize supporters in *just* those states, without unnecessarily bothering the rest of its supporters, who couldn't have as concrete an impact on elections in different states.

To mobilize supporters, OFA first sent out messages to *only* those in the relevant states, asking them if they were interested in helping out. As just one example, for the Wisconsin campaign, OFA texted people within Wisconsin:

> OFA Wisconsin is organizing this weekend to support Democratic candidates in the August 9th recall elections. Can you join us? Reply ACT to help.

OFA's initial contact message was a smart way to immediately segment out only those who wanted to get involved in *this* election. The Obama campaign mobile list is full of people who joined for numerous reasons. Some may be passionate about politics at the local level; some may just be Obama fans. Just as OFA didn't want to bother citizens in Wyoming with an election in Wisconsin, it also did not want to bother those who had no interest in the local recall with further messages of engagement. By asking users to positively reply to its message, it immediately segmented out only those people who had actively expressed an interest in this specific action.

When users replied back agreeing to participate in the outreach, OFA would then direct them to phone banks near them, where they could more concretely help the election effort. Texts like the following one went out for numerous phone banks, within a 10-mile radius around the relevant zip code:

> Help OFA Wisconsin volunteers organize around the recall elections. Join us tomorrow at 9am at 123 Main Street, Oshkosh.

Then, as the election neared, OFA could direct voters to the correct polling place:

> Don't forget to get out and vote for Democrat Kathy Hochul in tomorrow's special election. Polls are open from 6am-9pm. Find your polling place:

The text also included a link to send users to a web page where they could input their name and zip code and find out where they needed to go to vote.

OFA's mobile outreach around the recall elections is a great example of an organization using data to find a one-to-one opportunity. All politics is local, as the saying goes, and the entire national list of Obama supporters would not be interested in a Wisconsin election. So the first step for the campaign was to send a message *just* to those involved in the recall election, and see if they were interested. Once OFA had permission to further engage these users, it could send precisely targeted messages to convenient local phone banks that made it simple for volunteers to get involved. Then, to drive votes, it helped its supporters find the closest polling places to them.

Organizing for America's mobile campaign also drives local action in order to obtain national results. During last year's bitter Congressional fight over raising the debt ceiling, OFA wanted to stage rallies across the country to let Congress know where the American people stood. Its challenge was how to organize hundreds of local rallies from one centralized database.

The answer, of course, was text messaging. OFA sent out 500 separate locally targeted messages to its supporters around the country, giving each group precise instructions on where they could go to get involved. By turning a national movement into a convenient local activity, Organizing for America found the one-to-one opportunities to get its supporters involved.

Other Types of Data from a Mobile Campaign

Engaging your members based around their addresses is just the beginning of the ways in which you can use mobile data to find the one-to-one opportunities. With a mobile campaign, you can ask for *any* kind of data.

When the Sundance Film Festival signed up members for its mobile list, it asked its registrants whether they were a director, a member of the media, or a volunteer. It then used that information to send out relevant updates about after parties, press conferences, and special screenings.

Martha Stewart Weddings magazine ran a campaign that targeted newly engaged women not around their zip code or interest, but around *time*. Specifically, the campaign was based around the bride-to-be's wedding date. The magazine developed a flight of text messages that were automatically sent out based on each individual bride's schedule, working backward from her special day.

The messages included tips such as "practice your smile in the mirror BEFORE the cameras start clicking that day." And they also included sponsored recommendations for flowers and footwear, targeted around when the bride-to-be needed to be considering those crucial issues.

By relaying information based around this important life milestone, the Martha Stewart campaign took what could be a general appeal to "brides" and made it incredibly specific to each individual bride. In a future chapter you'll see how similar schedule-based messaging is revolutionizing the healthcare industry.

Some organizations also target their users based around the past actions they've taken within a campaign. Chapter 1 described how, when Reform Immigration For America wanted to reach out to its "top shelf" activists to throw house parties, it only messaged members who had made numerous advocacy calls on its behalf. (And how it later learned that throwing a house party was not necessarily a "top shelf" action so much as it was a *different* sort of action.)

Public Radio International's radio show *The World* engages in a simpler form of targeting based on past actions. Once a week, *The World* runs a geography quiz that asks a question such as the following:

Geo Quiz: Name the northernmost country of Central America. They're singing the national anthem there today, Independence Day! Text us your answer!

The show asks the question on-air, but also texts it out to its mobile list in advance to engage its audience before the show.

However, *The World* only texts out the answer (Belize, in this case) to those people who actually responded to the question. That may sound like a no-brainer—obviously, you only tell the answer to the people who respond. But using traditional forms of media, there wouldn't be a simple way to automatically exclude the people who weren't interested in your question to begin with.

Using Multiple Fields of Data for Truly Personal Targeting

The examples in the previous section relate the stories of how mobile campaigns can use a piece of information they've learned to better find opportunities to engage their users. OFA targets its users around their location. Sundance targets them around their career. *The World* targets them around whether or not they answered a question.

Some organizations, however, don't just use *one* piece of data. With a mobile campaign, you can target your messaging based on a *multitude* of criteria. For example, you could send a message just to men over the age of 45 named Charlie living within 10 miles of downtown Detroit who are passionate about strawberry ice cream. Combining multiple fields of data to engage your users lets you find truly personal opportunities.

Labor unions, for example, are some of the most innovative and extensive users of mobile engagement campaigns. That's because text messaging is uniquely useful for the unions. Text messaging allows unions to reach people that do not have consistent access to e-mail or the Internet, such as workers on job sites. Labor workers may not sit in front of a computer, but they will have their cell phones in their pockets.

Furthermore, unions often need a reliable way to send critical member communications as they occur. They need to keep their membership as informed as possible about negotiations and strikes so that their members can know whether or not to go to work. For example, when the Communications Workers of America (CWA) was caught in all-night negotiations with AT&T Mobility, they kept their members up-to-date by sending the blast:

> Parties agree to stop clock. Significant progress on some issues. Report to work as scheduled. Bargaining thru night. Your voices being heard. Updates when news breaks.

But labor unions want to do more than just keep their members informed. They want to keep them actively engaged in union activities such as meetings, rallies, and support of friendly candidates. They also want to offer opportunities and services to their dedicated members.

To create personal appeals, unions message their members based on criteria including where they're located, what language they speak, what their jobs are—and sometimes a combination of all three.

LIUNA, the Laborers' International Union of North America, for example, sends messages in English, Polish, and Spanish, depending on the audience. Those messages could be anything from a reminder about a member meeting to an update during an event that "The hospitality suite will be open for lunch at 11:45 a.m."

One recent LIUNA message targeted just the Spanish-speaking members of its Local 78 in New Jersey. Or, when LIUNA needed to find a Spanish-speaking shop steward in New York with an Amtrak license for a job opportunity, it was able to send a message to *just* that group of its members.

One of the classic rules of broadcast advertising is that if people have an opportunity to say "that's not me" to an ad, then you've already lost them. The kind of extreme targeting that LIUNA enacts flips that dictum on its head. The opportunities the union offers by targeting *just* Spanish-speaking shop stewards in New York are so incredibly specific that the recipients cannot *help* but see how the message is related to them.

DoSomething.org is another group that uses multiple sources of data to craft meaningful opportunities for its users. As previously mentioned, the Jonas Brothers gave the organization a national shout-out during their concert for President Obama's inauguration. VH1's Save the Music campaign was staged in partnership with DoSomething.org. And, of course, DoSomething.org maintains an active Facebook page.

But DoSomething.org really distinguishes itself in the way it uses data to create concrete activist opportunities for its audience. When members sign up for its mobile campaign, Do Something asks them both for their address and for the issues that matter most to them. Then, twice a month, DoSomething.org sends a text to each of its members with volunteer activities they can do right in their local communities, targeted around those areas of interest.

As a result, Do Something members only receive messages about the subjects they're passionate about—and in a way that allows them to take immediate action. By engaging its members around the one-to-one opportunities that matter most to them, DoSomething.org can mobilize an army of young people to do good in their local communities.

How One Campaign Used Data for In-Depth Analysis

Reform Immigration For America is perhaps the leader among nonprofits in using data to refine its messaging. As described earlier, it used the knowledge it learned from its "STOP" mistake to test out the different ways that different cultures respond to opt-out messaging. It also uses mobile data to target just its most active members.

As you can probably guess from those examples, RI4A is extensively data-driven. It rigorously tests every aspect of its campaign. It uses its mobile data not only to learn about its audience, but also to learn about the very nature of mobile engagement.

For one example, RI4A experimented to find the best way to structure a text message. As its landmark white paper, *Reform Immigration with Your Cell Phone*, describes it:

> We performed a test to determine the optimal placement of the call to action. Three options were tested: the beginning (to see if users would just call in right away, on our word alone), the end (our traditional formulation), or the middle (splitting the difference, providing a little information but still keeping the number above the fold).[2]

Here were the messages used—Beginning:

> Immigration alert: Reply CALL or 866-536-8629 - Republican senators wrote bill w/NO reform, only more of the same. Tell your senator: oppose border-only bill!

Middle:

> Immigration alert: Republican senators wrote bill w/NO reform, only more of the same. Reply CALL or 866-961-4293—Tell your senator: oppose border-only bill!

End:

> Immigration alert: Republican senators wrote bill w/NO reform, only more of the same. Tell your senator: oppose border-only bill! Reply CALL or 866-974-8813

We sent each message to a similar (though not identically sized) universe, and saw a statistically significant difference in response rates (see Table 4.1):

Table 4.1 **English Structure Test Results**

	Sent	Called	Action Rate
Beginning	5079	296	5.8%
Middle	7316	433	5.9%
End	5904	295	5.0%

We have a 98% confidence level that having the call to action in the middle of the English message is better than having it at the end (and a 94% confidence level on having it in the beginning)—while there's still some margin of error on beginning versus middle, we chose to make middle the standard based on both the slightly better result and the more intuitive structure—it's easier to break up a message than to lead with the number before a call to action begins.

Results on the Spanish side were exactly opposite, interestingly enough (see Table 4.2):

Table 4.2   **Spanish Structure Test Results**

	Sent	Called	Action Rate
Beginning	12857	598	4.7%
Middle	14869	609	4.1%
End	14487	837	5.8%

This might be a function of the nature of our Spanish supporters, or of the Spanish language itself. It's interesting that splitting the ask performs so much worse in Spanish than in English—evidentially, the two sentences work much better together in Spanish.

We've quoted at length to give you a window into the extensive and thoughtful data analysis that the RI4A has applied to its campaign—and a glimpse into how to arrange your own text messages. By using the data to determine even the structure of its messages, RI4A seeks to reach its users in the way that is most likely to get them to act.

RI4A has applied a similar analysis to every step of its campaign. For another example, one of RI4A's primary goals is to generate advocacy calls. Because RI4A uses a mobile CRM, it can keep track of every call made, how long it lasted, and who made it.

RI4A wanted to gain a window of insight into its less-involved users and find ways to transform them into more active participants. One of the things it wanted to know was why a person would make just *one* advocacy call. In some ways, it was more understandable why people would make *no* advocacy calls—they just weren't interested in making phone calls. But to make *one* advocacy call suggested a willingness to make phone calls, without the proper engagement following an initial spark.

To look deeper into users' motivation, RI4A compared its demographic of single-callers (some 30,000 members of its list) with the dates those callers joined the campaign. What it discovered was that the single-callers most often joined right in the lead-up to a major action—for example, petitioning Congress around important pro-immigration legislation. That made a fair amount of intuitive sense, as a person is most likely to be most enthusiastic about an advocacy campaign shortly after he or she joins, and right around the time that major legislation is dominating headlines and arousing strong emotions.

Another theory it considered, however, was that "the paid promotion we conducted more aggressively in the early spring of 2010 did not bring in quality members at the same rate as organic pass-along." Essentially, RI4A's discovery relates back to the initial example of "AD1" versus "AD2." Getting new members to join is only half the battle—you then need to get them to take action on your behalf.

RI4A still felt that the promotion was worthwhile, however. Every new member is a potential activist. And if the RI4A campaign can use its commitment to data to craft the perfect text messages, perhaps it can inspire even the least engaged new users to take action on its behalf.

How a Text Messaging Campaign Compares to Contextual Advertising

That last point takes us to the final topic of this chapter—how a contextual advertising campaign, such as Google's AdSense or Facebook's ads, compares to a text engagement campaign.

Boiled down to its basics, a campaign with Google AdSense lets you select certain keywords. When people doing Google searches type in those keywords, your ad surfaces on their web page. If they click your ad, you pay a certain amount to Google, and the user is taken to your website.

Like a mobile campaign, AdSense tracks every click. Using AdSense, you can see how many users are entering your site. You can see what actions they are taking. And, if you have a very clear metric for "conversion"—such as purchasing a product on an e-commerce website or filling out a form to inquire more about your company—you can see which ads most concretely convert leads. You can then calculate that against the amount of money you are spending for your campaign.

AdSense can be a very valuable and data-heavy way to drive traffic to your website. But the difference between an AdSense campaign and a mobile campaign is that you have no way to follow up directly with the people based on that data. In a mobile campaign, your users have given you permission to contact them again. AdSense, like so much of digital engagement, only provides you aggregate statistics.

Yes, you could tailor your ads, based on what you learn, to have a more effective campaign. In that way, you are better engaging the entire Internet audience. But you are not better engaging any single user. With AdSense, as with a restaurant walk-in, you're relying on one brief interaction to immediately lead to a sale.

A mobile campaign makes it easier for someone to join your audience, and then makes it easier for you to reach out to that person. By continued engagement, tailored across a wealth of data, you can find numerous one-to-one opportunities with your users—and build a truly one-to-one relationship.

In the next chapter, you'll see how, once that relationship has been established, you can inspire your users to take specific actions on your behalf.

STEP 3:

INSPIRE

ACTION

One short message never changed anyone's mind. No Coke drinker ever switched to Pepsi after reading 160 characters on a screen; no Republican ever voted Democrat because the Democrats sent him or her a text. But among those with the *intention* to vote or the curiosity to branch out from usual buying habits, a reminder at the right time can make all the difference between a forgotten impulse and a completed action. It can inspire the reminded person to make a purchase, express a preference, share personal information, or take other action for personal, political, or financial well-being.

To put it another way, integrated mobile campaigns can get the practical results that traditional marketing, these days, can only dream about. As advertising guru Jon Bond explains:

> We [advertisers] used to buy "eyeballs," meaning just the opportunity to have your ad seen. Now we are getting smart and talking about actually getting the consumer to do something about the ad, or at least to think about doing something about the ad.

In this chapter, we'll explore the ways integrated mobile campaigns get people off the couch and into action. We'll start with a few key ideas from the new hybrid science of behavioral psychology and economics (as described in Richard H. Thaler and Cass Sunstein's *Nudge* and Dan Ariely's *Predictably Irrational*) that shed light into how people make their day-to-day decisions. And we'll show how text reminders not only compel the recipient to read (almost always within 15 minutes) about a new opportunity, but to take action on that opportunity.

What action might that be? Anything they meant to do, but didn't: purchasing an item just now back in stock; confirming an appointment that was already forgotten; springing for the upgrade because now they have the frequent flier miles; providing feedback on a previous purchase or experience; sending a message to an elected official; and much more.

For political and advocacy groups, a text message can be a simple way to inspire their constituents to take one of the most essential actions of all: voting.

Text Out the Vote

What is the cheapest, most effective way to get voters to go to the polls? Political insiders had their suspicions, but it took collaboration by researchers at Princeton University, the University of Michigan, Working Assets (now CREDO Mobile), and three prominent voter registration organizations to confirm it. Door-to-door canvassing can plump turnout by 7 to 9 percent, but at the cost of $30 per vote. "Quality" phone calls can also boost turnout by 4 to 5 percent, but at a cost of

$20 per vote. By contrast, voters who received text message reminders to vote the day before the 2006 elections were 4.2 percent more likely to vote than voters who didn't—and messages that were concise and to the point produced even higher turnout—*and the cost per vote generated was $1.56,* drastically cheaper than every other mobilization technique.

Get-out-the-vote campaigns succeed or fail on the third of the four steps: inspire action. If you can reach likely supporters in a way they want to be reached, just a simple reminder can change an election. If you can't reach them when their vote matters most, or if you can only reach them in ways that annoy and irritate them (like the home telephone ringing all day long with calls from different volunteer organizations), then those supporters might as well not exist.

"The youth vote matters—18- to 31-year-olds will represent more than one-third of the electorate by 2015, and what this study shows is that we have another powerful tool in our toolkit to turn them out to the polls," said Ellynne Bannon, director of the Student PIRGs' New Voters Project, one of the groups involved in the study.[1]

Text-based campaigns can be simultaneously effective and inexpensive not just because text messaging is an efficient technology but also because it's a communication form that's keeping pace with changing lifestyles. Using text messaging intelligently allows organizations to reconnect with an audience they were in danger of losing.

Young people, for example, frequently register to vote just before elections, so their names don't appear on the rolls campaigns traditionally used to organize their outreach efforts.

They change addresses often, and many don't use landlines. In fact, by 2006, some 25 percent of Americans under the age of 25 used a mobile phone exclusively, and that trend is accelerating. It's not just young people: at the time of the 2008 presidential election, 30 percent of the American public was mobile-only. That's a huge portion of the population that traditional get-out-the-vote efforts can no longer reach.

Reaching the Teenage Audience— for Voting or Anything Else

The shift toward cell phones is more than just a technological upgrade. The *way* young people communicate is evolving too. Now that they have the choice, young people increasingly prefer being contacted via "passive" outreach—mobile and e-mail, for example—versus a phone call or a knock on the door that requires active conversation with a stranger. In a survey after the voter registration study, 59 percent of participants said they found the text message reminder helpful, and only 1 percent indicated that they were less likely to vote after receiving the message. Mobile was not just an efficient technology for this campaign. It was the right lifestyle choice for the people the campaign needed to reach, and it signaled an understanding of their lives and a respect for their preferences.

In fact, a recent Pew poll suggests that text messaging is not just *another* way to reach people, as Ellynne Bannon commented five years ago. Text messaging is increasingly becoming the *only* way people want to be reached. In the poll, 31 percent of the people who text said "they preferred texts to talking on the phone."[2]

Although 31 percent may seem small—after all, it's not even a majority—it's fairly incredible that a technology that's only been widely adopted for the past few years is already replacing the hallowed phone call, the hallmark of communications for more than a century. And, in fact, a majority (55 percent) of those who have heavily adopted text messaging prefer texting to talking.

The Pew poll is supported by recent data from comScore, whose report on 2010 digital trends shows that total web e-mail usage is down 8 percent in the past year—and down 59 percent among people between the ages of 12 and 17. E-mail use also declined 18 percent among 25- to 35-year-olds.[3]

If you have teenage friends or relatives, you no doubt have some anecdotal evidence of your own. Send an important e-mail that requires a timely response, and it's liable to languish unchecked in their inbox for days or weeks.

So if teens aren't checking their e-mail, how do you reach them? Maybe listen to Mark Zuckerberg. In 2010, when he introduced Facebook's reinvented messaging system, he said:

> High school kids don't use e-mail, they use SMS a lot. People want lighter weight things like SMS and IM to message each other.[4]

As this data suggests, maintaining a connection with an ever-changing target audience requires an understanding of both the available technologies and the changing habits and preferences that new technologies make possible. If people *prefer* to receive communications using SMS, who are we to deny them that?

Now try sending a text to your teenage nephew or cousin. You'll probably get a response before you even put your phone back into your pocket.

Mobile Reminders and Behavior Change

It's not just young people who can be motivated by mobile messages—particularly text messages . As more and more healthcare organizations are discovering, mobile can be a powerful tool for changing people's behaviors and encouraging healthy lifestyles.

One new study out of Columbia University shows that mobile messaging can be a great way to remind parents to get their children vaccinated. Dr. Melissa Stockwell, an assistant professor at Columbia, used text messaging to remind minority, low-income families about flu vaccinations. Her results show that text messages can help keep families healthy.

According to an article at the PediatricSuperSite, a group of parents received weekly text messages that reminded them about the importance of vaccinations and directed them to local clinics. Children of parents that got the texts were 7 to 9 percent more likely to receive the vital vaccinations than the control group. "Even that could make a real difference if used in a large population," Dr. Stockwell said.[5]

Traditional methods of outreach have had a lot lower impact. The study's control group only received "an automated phone reminder and fliers posted in the community office." That's just the kind of white noise that families are used to tuning out.

Mobile Commons is working on a similar reminder program with New York Presbyterian Hospital and the Harlem Health Promotion Center, called Project STAY (Services to Assist Youth). Project STAY's major focus is to provide ongoing care for several dozen HIV-positive adolescents and young adults, as well as other youth without a medical home—with a primary emphasis on sexual and reproductive health. As part of that campaign, the program sends appointment and medication reminders to young adults confronting an array of medical issues ranging from eye exams to birth control to HPV. For those young people who need reminders for their clinic appointments, the system sends out notifications three days before and on the day of the appointment. These notifications include the contact information for the clinic in case the patient needs to cancel or reschedule her treatment—or even just as a reminder of where to go at the appointment's time.

The system also sends out medication reminders—at a time of the young person's choosing. For young women using a Nuva ring, it sends weekly reminders, and on day 21 of the 28-day cycle, it reminds them to take out the ring: "Reminder to take out your ring! Please text OK to let us know you got this message and took care of business." Then on day 28, it sends a follow-up: "Reminder to put your new ring in. Please text OK to let us know you got this message and took care of business."

Text messaging has the potential to solve one of the most persistent medical problems: patient nonadherence. Many people believe that the burden of medicine is diagnosing illnesses and then developing treatments that can cure them. But one of the most common problems that doctors face is that patients just don't take their medicines.

Writing almost a decade ago in the *Wall Street Journal*, Amy Dockser Marcus described "the real drug problem: forgetting to take them."[6] Marcus cites a report from the World Health Organization that shows that only about half the global population actually follows their doctors' advice about which medicines to take. These failures can lead to chronic health problems and even death. Marcus in particular cites the problem with antiretroviral therapies (ARTS) for AIDS, which have notoriously complex regimens associated with them:

> Trials of antiretroviral therapies, for instance, have proved effective in suppressing the AIDS virus in as many as 95 percent of participating patients. But in the routine of daily life—when patients are less vigilant about following doctors' orders—the reported rates of suppression drop to the 40 to 50 percent range. Doctors believe the discrepancy is one important reason why so many people still continue to die from AIDS.

It's a lethal problem—but one against which mobile messaging is showing promising results. In November 2010, the *Lancet* ran a study on the effects of an SMS campaign in Kenya that focused on increasing patients' adherence to their antiretroviral therapies. Selected patients at three HIV clinics in Kenya received weekly SMS messages from a clinic nurse. The result was that "Patients who received SMS support had significantly improved ART adherence and rates of viral suppression compared with the control individuals."[7] Put simply, the text message reminders were effective and had demonstrable results.

Another study in 2009, from Mount Sinai Hospital in New York, showed that text messaging did not just increase drug adherence in liver transplant patients. It concretely led to better outcomes. According to the *New York Times*, "non-adherence . . . is the most important cause of organ rejection in long-term transplant survivors."[8] Teenagers are at a particular risk because—being teenagers—they're more likely to take their medications at the wrong time or forget to take them altogether.

Before text messaging, adherence interventions were clunky and ineffective. As the *New York Times* describes it:

> One potential solution, for example, had a clinician first identifying teenage patients who had been non-adherent, then increasing the frequency of their clinic visits and lecturing them about the importance of taking medications.

And there's nothing that quite improves a teenager's performance like punishments and lectures!

The study found that text messaging increased the likelihood that the patients would take their medicine. And as a result, fewer of the patients rejected the transplanted livers. "While 12 of the young people experienced rejection episodes in the previous year, only two did during the study."

According to Dr. Tamir Miloh, who is the lead author of the study, the text messages allowed the teenagers to feel like they were in control of their own choices—but also gave the parents a degree of oversight.

SMS's restricted character count—160 characters—can sometimes seem like an obstacle to communicating information. Certainly, there's nothing intuitive about communicating complex medical information in tiny bite-sized chunks. But as mentioned earlier, we've found that restriction can be a blessing in disguise. It forces both marketers and medics to communicate their message in a digestible format. That's about as much attention as people are willing to devote in their media-glutted lives. You may not get people to read a flyer or an e-mail, but they will give you 10 seconds when they glance at their phones. That's enough time to remind someone to take his or her medicine. That's a foot in the door that can save lives.

Dr. Miloh sums up the long-term possibilities for texting:

> This kind of communication can only help to enhance the relationship between patients and their clinicians.
>
> Clinicians have been hesitant to deal with adolescent patients who were nonadherent because they thought these teenagers could not change. But for the most part, these were intelligent kids who said they did not want us to give up on them. They simply had busy schedules and forgot to take their medications or to follow up with their doctors and nurses.

Text messaging can provide just the kind of reminders those teenagers need.

Mobile Messaging and Impulse Control

As effective as mobile can be in reminding people to *do* something, it can be equally effective in reminding them *not* to do something. One of the most promising ways that healthcare groups are using SMS to inspire action is actually to inspire self-control. One use that has generated a lot of attention is the power of mobile to help smokers quit.

At Mobile Commons, we've worked on smoking cessation campaigns with the New York City Department of Health and Mental Hygiene and the Louisville Metro Department of Public Health and Wellness. The way it works is that users text in their target quit day when they join. Then—similar to the *Martha Stewart Weddings* campaign discussed in the last chapter—they receive a flight of messages scheduled around their unique date. Unlike the Martha Stewart campaign, however, these messages are not advice on where to buy the most festive bridal bouquets. Instead, messages of encouragement alternate with tips, such as "meet, greet, and defeat your triggers, don't hide from them."

That may not immediately *sound* like the type of inspirational message that would overwhelm the notoriously persistent urge to smoke. But it worked. The data overwhelmingly showed that the text messages helped people stop smoking.

- Among 26- to 35-year-olds, 47 percent successfully quit, compared to 35 percent in the control group.

- Among males, 43 percent successfully quit when receiving the texts, compared to 29 percent of the control group.

- Most impressively, among heavy smokers, 53 percent successfully quit when receiving texts, compared to 25 percent of the control group.

That's more than *twice as many* heavy smokers who were able to quit thanks to receiving SMS messages.[9]

There have been a lot of other recent studies that backs up that data. Two recent studies, from the University of Oregon and UCLA, showed that text messaging can "measure and intervene in urges people have during smoking cessation programs."[10]

Scientists at the two universities used functional magnetic resonance imaging (fMRI) on 27 smokers to map the areas of the brain where they control their impulses. The goal was to gain a better understanding of the way in which people struggle to overcome their cravings. The scientists described the constant struggle against temptation as "a war that consists of a series of momentary self-control skirmishes."

The researchers then asked the smokers to text in their habits over the following three weeks, as the smokers struggled to quit. The studies found that real-time texting dramatically increases the accuracy of people's reporting and can serve as an effective tool for helping them quit altogether. According to the report:

> Text messaging may be an ideal delivery mechanism for tailored interventions because it is low-cost, most people already possess the existing hardware and the messages can be delivered near-instantaneously into real world situations.

The report hints at a future world of radical targeting—where everyone's ability to resist temptation is calibrated and accounted for. (For example, the text messages revealed that the study participants who had "the most activity in the key regions of their brains" also were "the most likely to resist their cravings to smoke.") Similarly, though on a slightly less futuristic note, part of what makes current nonsmoking campaigns so effective is that messages can be scheduled according to each individual's personal quit date. As discussed at length in the last chapter, a personalized message of encouragement has a lot more relevance than a broadcast message receivers can easily ignore.

More and more projects around the world are discovering the radical possibilities that an SMS behavior change campaign can provide. In an article in the *Epidemiologic Reviews* entitled "Text Messaging as a Tool for Behavior Change in Disease Prevention and Management," authors Heather Cole-Lewis and Trace Kershaw discuss the impact of SMS on healthcare globally. For example, "In South Africa, Project Masiluleke uses text messaging to increase rates of testing for tuberculosis and human immunodeficiency virus (HIV) and to provide counseling for patients."[11]

In a "study of studies," Cole-Lewis and Kershaw run through a number of recent tests from around the world that chart the efficacy of these SMS engagement programs.

In France, a study in diabetes management chose 30 type 1 diabetics with poor control and sent them text messages with medical advice. The study found a marked increase in the "quality of life," as determined by a survey.

In South Korea, a similar study involved nurses sending out text messages to 60 type 2 diabetics. That study found significant health benefits for the group that received the text messages.

Perhaps the most remarkable data came out of an obesity program in Finland. The program sent "automated, targeted, weight-specific tailored text messages to reduce daily food intake, increase physical activity, encourage daily weight recording, and provide instant feedback" to 126 overweight adults aged 25 to 44. After a year of receiving the messages, the study found that the intervention group lost *more than four times as much weight* as the control group.

Additionally, the authors found that text messages were actually more beneficial than other types of digital intervention. They write, "These studies found that text reminders result in increased frequency of blood glucose monitoring when compared with e-mail reminders and that hemoglobin A1c levels decreased when compared with an Internet-based monitoring system." In short, of all the different types of digital reminders, text messaging seemed to have the greatest positive impact.

Or to translate that back into academicese: "Increased communication, accountability, and reinforcement created by text messaging may increase the likelihood of remembering the changes that one should be making."

Free Offers and the Science of Behavioral Economics

Chapter 3 discussed how the Sacramento Kings and the ARCO Arena built an impressive mobile list by reaching out to a captive audience and providing them compelling opportunities. The Kings would induce fans to text to join its list by offering discounts on tickets and exclusive offers to events like player appearances.

Not surprisingly, free offers are another powerful way to inspire people to take action. At a UWC Mixed Martial Arts event, for example, the announcers told the assembled audience that they could text in for a chance to win ringside seats. The message was repeated throughout the event on the arena scoreboard. Over 20 percent of the thousands of people texted in, and over 80 percent of those provided their e-mail address when asked for it. One lucky winner was given two ringside seats.

At the end of the event, the entire list of people who had texted in to win the tickets was thanked for attending and encouraged to buy merchandise on their way out, all via text message. When tickets went on sale for the *next* Mixed Martial Arts event in the area, both the e-mail and SMS lists received messages asking them to buy tickets. The UWC turned one offer of two free tickets into an ongoing mobile engagement with thousands of people.

More and more scientists are starting to study why "free" offers motivate us to the extent that they do—and all the other psychology behind our often strange choices. MIT Professor Dan Ariely, a researcher in the new science of behavioral economics, explores the science behind our economic behaviors. He's gone so far as to negotiate candy trades with children trick-or-treating during Halloween. He found that children will choose a free candy bar over a candy bar "trade," even if the trade actually benefits them more.[12] Ariely believes that "'FREE!' gives us such an emotional charge that we perceive what is being offered as immensely more valuable than it really is."[13]

Ariely and other behavioral economists are examining the decisions people make from a psychological perspective. And they've come to realize that people's purchasing and consumption decisions are not always—or even often—guided by the rational self-interest that free market economics assumes.

As with the traditional study of psychology, this new behavioral economic research shows that people's decisions are often based on biases, laziness, fear, and incomplete information. In one example, Ariely and a colleague "asked students at M.I.T.'s Sloan School of Management to write the last two digits of their Social Security number at the top of a piece of paper." They then asked the students to write down the amount of money they'd be willing to spend on a nice bottle of wine, a less-nice bottle, a book, and a box of chocolates. When Ariely looked at the results, he saw that the students' opinions had been directly influenced by their social security numbers. As the *New Yorker* describes it,

> The students whose Social Security number ended with the lowest figures—00 to 19—were the lowest bidders. For all the items combined, they were willing to offer, on average, sixty-seven dollars. . . . The pattern continued up to the highest group—80 to 99—whose members were willing to spend an average of a hundred and ninety-eight dollars . . . for the same items.[14]

The effect, according to Ariely, is called "anchoring," and what it means is that to a certain extent, the prices you see determine the price you're willing to pay—irrespective of the actual value of the goods. As the *New Yorker* summarizes, "What if the numbers on the board [at Starbucks] are influencing your sense of what a Double Chocolaty Frappuccino is worth?"

That's just one example of the ways in which people twist information in the world around them to make (predictably) irrational decisions. One of the most useful distinctions behavioral economists make is between people's "hot" and "cold" or "cool" states. As *Wikipedia* describes it, "In our cool state we make rational long-term decisions, whereas in our hot state we give in to immediate gratification and put off our decisions made in the cool state."[15] Or, as David Berreby writes in a *New York Times* review of *Predictably Irrational*:

> Yes, you have a rational self, but it's not your only one, nor is it often in charge. A more accurate picture is that there are a bunch of different versions of you, who come to the fore under different conditions. We aren't cool calculators of self-interest who sometimes go crazy; we're crazies who are, under special circumstances, sometimes rational.[16]

One famous experiment where Ariely demonstrated the difference was by testing male UC Berkeley students' responses to sexually charged questions when they were in a "rational" state of mind, imagining their answers when they were aroused. He then asked the same set of questions again when they were highly aroused, as stimulated by Internet pornography. Questions ranged from "would [you] find women's shoes erotic?" to "could you enjoy sex with someone you hated" and "would you always use a condom?" The computers were covered in Saran wrap.

"In every case," Ariely writes, "Our bright young participants answered the questions very differently when they were aroused from when they were in a 'cold' state."[17] Their likelihood of performing one of the "somewhat odd sexual activities" or immoral acts was twice as high when they were in an aroused state, compared to a "cool" state.

The study shows a lot more than just that college boys are willing to be reckless when they're in extreme conditions. The broader lesson is that people have trouble predicting their own behaviors. It's easy to plan out your life along the good intentions you have when you're in your "cold" state. However, those noble ideas are often quickly discarded as soon as your emotional state changes. The problem actually has a name in behavioral economics. It's called the "hot-cold empathy gap," a term coined by Carnegie Mellon University professor George Loewenstein.

Ariely's research can cast a light into why SMS reminders can be so effective. It may seem fairly obvious that if people are reminded to do something, they are more likely to do it. And that is indeed one excellent reason why SMS messages can work so well at crucial moments.

But there are often more psychologically complex motivations at play in people's avoidance strategies. For example, as Marcus wrote in the *Wall Street Journal*, the problems with drug adherence aren't only that people are forgetting to take their meds. There are a whole host of reasons at work:

Some of it is human nature, an inner rebellious voice that resists the doctor's orders. Many patients mean to take their pills but don't write down what the doctor says and end up not following the instructions properly. Others forget. . . .

But the major reason appears to be a fear of side effects. People don't like the way they feel when they take many drugs, so they simply stop taking them.[18]

Some people forget to take their medication. Some willfully neglect their medication out of short-term financial worries or fear of physical pain. Other nonadherers are just being willful.

In another experiment, Ariely designed a test in which it was incredibly easy to cheat. After the test was done, he simply asked people to self-report the number of answers they got correct. (Another group, the control, handed in their exams directly to the researcher.) However, before the test began, Ariely asked the students to write down one of two things. One group was asked to write down the names of 10 books they read in high school. The other group was asked to write down the Ten Commandments from the Bible.

The study found that the students who simply wrote down the names of books were inclined to cheat—reporting on average 33 percent more answers correct than the control group. But as for the students who wrote down the Ten Commandments? Ariely writes, "The results surprised even us: the students who had been asked to recall the Ten Commandments had not cheated at all."

The other interesting result of the test was that students who could only remember a few of the Commandments were just as disinclined to cheat as students who remembered all 10. The conclusion is that it wasn't necessarily rigorous religious instruction that led these students not to cheat. Rather, it was "the mere contemplation of a moral benchmark of some kind" that inspired their adherence to honesty.

That casts some light on why SMS reminders can be so useful in drug adherence or voting. They're an example of the "cool" mind intruding onto the "hot." Even in the middle of a hectic day, when people are beset by the quotidian dramas that make up so much of life, if they get a text message, it doesn't just remind them of the action. It also reminds them of the entire set of motivations that inspired that action.

Cole-Lewis and Kershaw, in their article in the *Epidemiologic Reviews*, suggest something similar at the conclusion of their article. "The process of text messaging itself," they write, "may tap important constructs (e.g., cues to action, reinforcement, social support) central to many behavioral theories even when the developer of the program did not explicitly base the content of the message on a theory."[19]

How a Text Message Can Be Even More Valuable than a "Nudge"

In their book *Nudge*, behavioral economists Richard H. Thaler and Cass Sunstein also confront the problem of people's predictably irrational decisions. They note that often people who are smokers or drinkers not only acknowledge that they are, and not only wish that they weren't—but they're actually willing to spend money to stop themselves from indulging in these behaviors.

"With respect to diet, smoking, and drinking, people's current choices cannot reasonably be claimed to be the best means of promoting their well-being. Indeed, many smokers, drinkers, and overeaters are willing to pay third parties to help them make better decisions,"[20] they write.

Thaler and Sunstein propose what they call a "nudge." Basically, it means for government and institutions to arrange people's environments so they make the best possible decisions. The most straightforward example that Thaler and Sunstein give is the idea of a school cafeteria. The cafeteria manager has the decision of where to place the different items, from the fruit to the sandwiches to the pudding. She can choose to place the desserts first in the line or list. She can put the fruit at eye level or on a higher shelf. By the way she arranges the cafeteria items, she can incline students to favor one item over another.

This isn't just a hypothetical. Thaler and Sunstein open up their book with an actual real-life example of Carolyn, a director of food services for a large city school system, who wanted to test out the optimal way to arrange the food. "Simply by rearranging the cafeteria, Carolyn was able to increase or decrease the consumption of many food items by as much as 25 percent."

Thaler and Sunstein argue that people in Carolyn's position should arrange the food in a way to encourage the healthiest possible choices. So, for example, Carolyn should put the fruit at eye level, rather than the candy.

In an interview with Democracy Now!, Sunstein lays out their thinking. "Ordinary people sometimes blunder. We sometimes have self-control problems. We sometimes don't have adequate information. We sometimes are too optimistic about our future, both as individuals and as nations, facing let's say hurricane or climate change or security threats. Sometimes the best approach government can take is a nudge, which doesn't require anyone to do anything, that can set up a situation or a context in a way that leads people and governments to make better decisions."[21]

Thaler and Sunstein engage in quite a bit of hand-wringing over the moral implications of a "nudge." They worry that "nudging" is inherently paternalistic. (In fact, they call their moral system "libertarian paternalism.") And while it's hard to argue against a lot of what Thaler and Sunstein propose (who could possibly complain about encouraging children to eat fresh fruit?), some worry that "nudge" might just nudge you down a slippery slope. "Nudging" could lead down a rabbit hole to even more oppressive and regulatory forms of government. As the *New Yorker* summarizes, "If the 'nudgee' can't be depended on to recognize his own best interests, why stop at a nudge? Why not offer a 'push,' or perhaps even a 'shove'?"

That may not be an academic question. After all, Cass Sunstein is a close confidant of President Obama. He was recently named administrator of the White House's Office of Information and Regulatory Affairs.

An SMS campaign can take a middle ground—providing people the information they need or the reminders to help exhibit self-control, without the fear of subconscious manipulation. The great thing in a mobile campaign is that you don't need to fret about "libertarian paternalism," since people are *choosing* to join. You don't need to go down the ethically sticky path of "nudging" people into making better decisions . . . if they're asking to be reminded.

When people sign up to get nonsmoking reminders, they are admitting that they do not have the willpower to quit smoking by themselves. When people sign up for medication reminders, they are admitting that sometimes their mind wanders. The "hot-cold empathy gap" is penetrated because now the "cold" self has the wherewithal to remind the "hot" self of all of his or her noble resolutions.

That's not just the case for healthcare reminders or voting decisions. Signing up for a commercial campaign can also be a method of accessing the kind of life you want to live. After all, many people choose the brands they support according to their personal values.

If someone receives a text from Nike reminding him or her to sign up for a relay race (as you'll see in Chapter 8), that can inspire positive action. Or if a busy homemaker gets a text from Martha Stewart Dinner Tonight that suggests a delicious meal option, that too can serve as a prompt toward a more fulfilling lifestyle. When WNYC asked its listeners to text in to its "snow map" and report the weather conditions, this enabled people to be more engaged citizens. Text reminders provide access to the civic and personal values that we may idealize in our "cold" states, but quickly become forgotten in our "hot."

The Alliance for Climate Education (ACE) made excellent use of this idea in its outreach. At rallies for the environment, when people are most inspired and enthused about its message, it asks people to text in one pledge about a way they will help the environment. For example, "I'll always turn off the lights when I leave the house."

Asking people to make a pledge is a great way to encourage them to support your mission. But the ACE knows that a pledge made in one emotional state can have limited impact in another. A week later, the alliance therefore follows up with a text message asking respondents whether or not they have lived up to their pledge. The text brings back the high emotion and inspiration of the rally and inserts it into the user's daily life. It's more than just a reminder, it's the impetus for change.

Mobile messaging has already radically reinvented the way we communicate. We're just beginning to see its potential in changing the way we live. The more we learn about the science of how people make their decisions, the more we can see the future utility of mobile engagement.

In the next chapter, we'll discuss how a mobile campaign can do more than just drive action—it can build actual relationships with the people you want to reach most.

STEP 4:
DEVELOP A
LONG-TERM
RELATIONSHIP

We are all so used to the marketing methods of major commercial events—new Hollywood movies, for example—that few consider how outdated and wasteful such approaches have become. When a major movie studio releases a film with blockbuster potential, it will spend vast amounts on traditional advertising, exposing everyone who goes to that kind of movie (and many people who don't) to previews and information in media old and new, from television and newspapers to web advertising and social network campaigns. It's not hard to understand why studios put so much into publicity—getting someone to see a movie in a theater is almost as demanding as getting him or her on a plane. The viewer has to commit to a time, arrange transportation to and from the theater, and increasingly, buy a ticket in advance.

This means that each viewer who makes it to a movie has revealed, by his or her behavior, a significant level of interest in and commitment to theatergoing in general and to a specific genre of movie in particular. If a patron is willing to see one

Jason Bourne movie in a theater, chances are the person would want see another, as well as other thrillers and perhaps other Matt Damon movies. He or she might be glad to receive information regularly about other films the studio is making with the same stars or director; might be willing to provide feedback about the advertising that drew him or her to the film and about the film itself; might show up for advance showings of future movies before reviews are out; and might buy movie-related merchandise such as clothes, soundtracks, DVDs, and video games.

Yet although every movie creates the potential for an ongoing commercial relationship between the studio and some of its customers, what do the studios and their marketers do when a viewer reveals this highly valuable information? Very little. They have no means to discover which viewers actually went to a given movie, what advertising reached them, whether they liked the movie they saw, or how to reach that person again in the future with offers of other movies he or she might want to see.

In the same way, the customer who needs a wedding dress this month will presumably need other dresses for other wedding-related events. She will probably take a honeymoon and continue to take vacations after that; she will have other parties to throw, a home to furnish, anniversaries and other milestones to celebrate, and many more reasons to return to the brands she associates with her wedding for decades to come. The same goes for the customer who needs a business suit, a pool cue, a packet of seeds, or any other purchase associated with an ongoing work or leisure activity. Every one of these customers, potentially, represents not just a single sale but also a highly qualified, long-term arrival in the seller's digital universe, ripe to begin a long-term digital relationship.

A mobile campaign can be a perfect way to capture information and set up a dialogue of continual engagement that will turn a one-off consumer transaction into a prolonged relationship—even into a lifetime of engagement. Throughout the previous chapters, we've already described a few ways that companies have used the knowledge gained from their mobile users to continually engage them around the subjects that matter to them most:

The ARCO Arena understood that someone who went to one game for the Sacramento Kings probably would be willing to go to another. Additionally, it realized that that person had expressed an interest in going not just to Kings games, but more generally, an interest in attending live events in the Sacramento area. Arena marketers therefore came to the conclusion, why not send people who join our list offers for other events at the stadium, like concerts? As a result, the arena developed a massive mobile list and earned as much as $10 to $12 in incremental revenue per person, per text broadcast.

St. Jude Children's Research Hospital built a bond with college students when it hosted its most active activists at its College Leadership Seminar in Memphis. But St. Jude realized that while the students might be enthusiastic about the St. Jude mission while they were at a training event in Memphis, they very well could become distracted once they returned to their hectic college lives. St. Jude therefore developed a campaign of ongoing communication that reminded the students about the urgency of the St. Jude mission—for example, it broadcast inspiring stories from St. Jude patients. St. Jude also specifically engaged the college leaders around fund-raising events by sending out encouraging messages of support.

Chapter 4 discussed *Martha Stewart Weddings*, which sends out tips and product offers targeted around recipients' wedding date. *Martha Stewart Weddings'* mobile campaign is a particularly excellent example of a smart way to take what you know about a person and build an ongoing relationship. *Martha Stewart Weddings* understood that a young bride-to-be planning her big day will have a fairly consistent list of needs: flower arrangements, shoes, a wedding dress. Therefore, it sends targeted messages that provide sponsored suggestions for ways to fulfill those needs—and make that special day even more magical. For example, one recent text message read:

> Nordstrom has the dress of your dreams, plus stunning looks for your wedding party and every occasion surrounding your special day. (http://shop.nordstrom.com/c/wedding-shop?cm_ven=fls&cm_cat=wedding_suite&cm_pla=msw&cm_ite=iotd_ad)

That web link at the end of that message takes the recipient directly to Nordstorm's wedding website. And because a mobile CRM can track every web click, *Martha Stewart Weddings* can see specifically what users are taking advantage of what offers and use that information to further target its outreach.

But the staff at *Martha Stewart Weddings* also understood that the most important way to build a relationship is to treat your target customer as more than an oversized wallet. They wanted to provide information to their mobile list that was useful even without driving to a purchasing opportunity. To that end, the magazine's editorial director, Darcy Miller, sends out weekly tips called "Darcy's Idea of the Week." The tips help young couples confront the issues that often arise in wedding planning. For example:

> Darcy's Tip: If you receive a gift at your engagement party, wait to open it. Gifts aren't required & other guests may feel awkward.

or

> Darcy's Tip: Make sure the dance floor is big enough—4–5 ft per guest is about right. For more tips visit www.martha stewartweddings.com.

By interweaving their sponsored suggestions with practical tips, *Martha Stewart Weddings* establishes itself as a trusted source and builds a connection that goes beyond a quick product offer. And as you can see, many of the tips drive the recipients back to the *Martha Stewart Weddings* website, where there are further opportunities to both engage the users and expose them to sponsored merchandise.

All of these companies took a single connection and developed it into a long-term relationship. This chapter will explore the dangers of using gimmicks that get new customers in the door but don't build those long-term relationships. It will look at the daily deal service Groupon and show that while companies who advertise with Groupon will often experience a surge in customers, those new one-off sales rarely convert to repeat business—and can often have a detrimental impact on the company. It will also consider a range of ways to convert short-term interest in products or services into lasting relationships. While the approaches and techniques vary among different companies and their unique needs, the overall goal is always the same: to become a trusted source, one the consumer looks forward to hearing from and feels inspired to ask questions that matter.

The Dangers of Gimmicks Without Relationship

If you're not familiar with Groupon, you probably haven't been paying much attention to the business news for the past two years. For a brief moment, the daily deals site seemed ready to revolutionize the world of local marketing—and it could very well rebound by the time this book is published in 2012. Yet for all the hype and excitement that Groupon generated in 2010, the actual impact the site had for the businesses that used it was more questionable.

The basic premise behind Groupon is, on its face, a very clever way to combine new local technology with old ideas about couponing and customer acquisition. The service e-mails out daily discounts to its members, targeted by zip code (and, more recently, also targeted around gender and buying history). But the deals come with a catch. They only take effect if a critical mass of people agree to them. According to the company's *Wikipedia* page:

The company offers one "Groupon" ("group coupon") per day in each of the markets it serves. The Groupon works as an assurance contract using ThePoint's [Groupon's predecessor] platform: if a certain number of people sign up for the offer, then the deal becomes available to all; if the predetermined minimum is not met, no one gets the deal that day. This reduces risk for retailers, who can treat the coupons as quantity discounts as well as sales promotion tools. Groupon makes money by keeping approximately half the money the customer pays for the coupon. For example, an $80 massage could be purchased by the consumer for $40 and then Groupon and the retailer would split the $40. That is, the retailer gives a massage valued at $80 and gets approximately $20 from Groupon for it. And the consumer gets the massage, in this example, from the retailer for which they have paid $40 to Groupon.[1]

From their first deal in October of 2008 (a half-price offer for pizzas) up through 2010, Groupon was exceedingly successful. Only 20 people took advantage of the site's first deal for half-off pizzas. In December 2008, Groupon had 400 responses. In December 2010, they had 44 million.

Consumers were eager to take advantage of discounted offers from local businesses. And merchants were excited at the opportunity to reach new customers. Groupon provided local businesses new ways to advertise within their communities without resorting to broadcast media. According to a *Wall Street Journal* article from December 2010, "Until Groupon came along, a small business—say, an independent yoga studio—was generally confined to advertising in newspapers, on the radio and online."[2]

By the end of 2010, everything seemed to be going perfectly for Groupon. The site had spawned competitors, like the Amazon-backed Living Social, but none of them seemed to threaten Groupon's growth or cultural cache. The *Journal* reported that "According to *Forbes* . . . the company is on pace to make $1 billion in sales faster than any other business, ever." The *New York Times* wrote a fawning puff piece over how Groupon's writers worked their literary magic to craft compelling offers— here quoting the site's editorial director, Aaron With:

> "We're mixing business with art and creating our own voice." [he said] The Voice. "This, Groupon says, is what subscribers respond to as much as the deal itself."[3]

When Google offered to buy the company for $6 billion dollars, Groupon turned down the offer, instead opting to issue an IPO with a valuation that reached as high as $30 billion.

What a difference a year makes. Whether it's the increased scrutiny caused by the company's IPO, or simply a question of more time having passed to analyze the site's benefits and drawbacks, the worm has turned for Groupon's fortunes. "The Internet coupon fad is shrinking faster than fat from a weightloss laser," writes the *New York Times*.[4] Groupon repeatedly delayed its public offering, and many of the Groupon clones are shuttering their businesses or reformulating their business plans. Even the writing staff who wrote the web copy feels stretched thin: "'We were used to small audiences, like blogs that we were the creators and the only readers of,' said Daniel Kibblesmith, a Groupon copywriter. 'Now it seems like an audience we can't wrap our heads around.'"

So what happened to Groupon? According to the *New York Times*, there was an inherent contradiction in what consumers were hearing and what the companies that were offering the deals were being told:

> The consumers were being told: You will never pay full price again. The merchants were hearing: You are going to get new customers who will stick around and pay full price. Disappointment was inevitable . . . .
>
> Contrary to what the company had maintained, it was not profitable in the traditional sense. Eighty percent of subscribers to Groupon's daily e-mails never bought a deal.[5]

Groupon's real fatal flaw was not just the high percentage of people who never actually used the site. Even worse for businesses than the consumers who weren't using Groupon were the consumers who *did* take advantage of the offers. Because of Groupon's high percentage from all coupon profits (upward of 50 percent), businesses often took a loss in fulfilling the daily coupons. That in itself is not disastrous. "Loss leaders" are a well-established practice in business—offering a product for below its cost in order to get new customers in the door, sell them other goods, and build your brand reputation.

The greater problem was that Groupon customers were often not repeat customers. They would come once for the daily deal—and then be off to the next merchant, in search of the next deal. As the *New York Times* writes, "Even worse from the merchants' point of view, the popularity of the coupon sites fed a relentless bargain-hunting mentality among customers that did not use them."

The site's promise had been that it would provide exposure for small businesses without the hefty costs of advertising. But a Groupon deal came with surprisingly hefty costs of its own, and the mirage of repeat customers rarely manifested.

The reason for that is fairly straightforward. The companies that were offering deals with Groupon never directly engaged the end consumer. The customers were Groupon's, their information was Groupon's—and when one Groupon deal was over, they moved on to the next Groupon deal. Merchants had no way of building a sustained relationship with these consumers beyond the one-off coupon. And the Groupon discounts were often offered at unprofitable margins.

In his book *Groupon: Why Deep Discounts Are Bad for Business*, Bob Phibbs discusses exactly this phenomenon. "The fallacy of trying to make Groupon or other online discount program users into your customer is the fact that *they are already someone else's customer*,"[6] he writes. Groupon's minimum usage requirements also only help to spread the word about *Groupon*—not about the merchant. Phibbs writes,

> They're going to tell their friends all about the site—*not you*—because they have to tell enough of their friends to get the "deal of the day." And suddenly you've been usurped, lost, moved to the back of the bus, seen as a loser because their new BFF gave them a deal you wouldn't.

Throughout this book, if there's been one continual mantra, it's been, learn as much as possible about your target user to build a sustained relationship with him or her. Through continual engagement, you can not only build a history of brand loyalty, but actually increase your profits. Groupon's business model flies in the face of that basic premise. By positioning itself between the end merchant and the target consumer, Groupon blocks actual relationships. In fact, recent data suggests that it encourages *dissatisfaction*.

A new study from researchers out of Boston University and Harvard looked at data from over 16,000 Groupon deals in 20 U.S. cities between January and July 2011. They juxtaposed that data against Yelp reviews from the relevant merchants. As MIT's *Technology Review* describes it, "They collected Yelp reviews—some 56,000 of them for 2,332 merchants who ran 2,496 deals—examining how merchant reputations changed before and after a Groupon deal:"[7]

> A Groupon deal seems to have an adverse impact on reputation as measured by Yelp ratings. Their analysis shows that while the number of reviews increases significantly due to daily deals, average rating scores from reviewers who mention daily deals are about 10% lower than scores of their peers.

There are numerous reasons why this could be the case. Consumers hunting bargains rather than the actual service being offered might have significantly less tolerance for the natural hiccups and inconveniences that most client-facing services

entail. Or they may simply have less interest in the given service. Regardless of the reasons, the consequences for merchants
are dire. Yelp ratings have been shown to have a concrete
impact on sales (one researcher showed that "a one-star increase
in the Yelp rating led to an increase of 5 percent to 9 percent in
revenue for independent restaurants").[8] By focusing their
attentions on consumers who are more interested in bargain
hunting than the business's actual services, merchants cost
themselves money, alienate their core clients (who can be frustrated at the deals that these newcomer customers are receiving), and may actually decrease long-term profitability.

Of course, it's very possible that in a year, Groupon will have
rebounded. It may have altered its business model and developed
a new way for local businesses to achieve more publicity and more
profit. But for now, the quick fix of Internet coupons seems to
have more dangerous and deleterious side effects than benefits.

Compare the impact of a Groupon coupon with a recent
coupon offer created by the Build-A-Bear Workshop. Build-A-
Bear lets children (or adults) customize and assemble their very
own teddy bears. They can choose the type of bear, its clothes
(from a sports jersey to a princess ensemble), accessories (ranging from purses to sunglasses to a bear-themed iPod), to the
sound the bear makes when you squeeze it. Founded by Maxine
Clark in 1997, Build-A-Bear has sold over 50 million bears in
over 400 stores across the globe a decade later.[9]

Maxine's innovation wasn't teddy bears—or even stores
where you could make your own teddy bear. It was in the way
that Build-A-Bear engages consumers. As Maxine writes, "We

decided to reinvent the idea of making your own stuffed animals for mall-based retailing. After all, Ray Kroc from McDonald's didn't invent hamburgers and Howard Schultz from Starbucks didn't invent coffee, they just invented how to sell more and how to sell it better."[10]

When Build-A-Bear wanted to drive sales and learn more about its users, it advertised a coupon offer. People were encouraged to text in to get a discount on Build-A-Bear purchases, as well as being entered in a drawing to receive a "Bear Buck$" gift card.

Twenty-three percent of the Build-A-Bear coupons were redeemed. That in itself is a remarkable rate of redemption for any coupon. More important, the Build-A-Bear coupons were offered at a sustainable price to drive profits, and the company did not have to split its earnings with anybody.

Build-A-Bear's coupons were profit drivers—but perhaps most significant, the Build-A-Bear mobile coupon drove people *to join the Build-A-Bear list.* Build-A-Bear made direct contact with everybody who texted in to receive the coupon. And when the company later followed up with its new list members to learn more information, 42 percent of them submitted their e-mail addresses.

Build-A-Bear established a direct relationship with its customers. It used its coupon to build mobile and e-mail lists with which it could easily contact people again. It reached out only to people who wanted a Build-A-Bear coupon—rather than people who just wanted *any* coupon. And it retained all the information for itself.

College Mobile Deals

Build-A-Bear's mobile campaign is a great example of how you can turn a coupon into a long-standing relationship. But Mobile Commons has worked on a project close to the Groupon model. In the spirit of full disclosure, we want to discuss that campaign and show that, while it never achieved the scale of Groupon, it did achieve more sustainable results.

College Mobile Deals (CMD) was the mobile extension of College Discount Cards, a business that started at Arizona State University and was dedicated to finding students discounted offers in their communities. Students who signed up for the mobile list would daily receive text messages with coupons to local retailers—especially restaurants, but also clothing merchants.

As the College Mobile Deals list grew into the thousands, conversion rates for the coupons remained amazingly high—30 percent at the high end, 5 percent on the low end. There were days when the coupons caused a line out the door for major franchises like Pizza Hut, Qdoba, and Papa John's. Here are a few of their sample offers:

Restaurant: Buy 1 Burrito GET THE 2ND BURRITO 4 ONLY $1.99! ($5 Savings!) Grab a friend, go 2 Restaurant & split the cost! Vld to 11pm!

CELEBRATE w/end of the year SALE Thur-Sun @ *Clothing Retailer* Show this text for: 35% OFF one non-denim item! OR: 25% OFF one denim item! Mens Clothing too!

$5 LARGE 1-TOPPING! (Pick up OR DELIVERY) @ *National Pizza Chain*. Min $10 Delivery. Delivery Extra. Call (480) 222-4500.

Within a few months, the business had grown to four campuses with hundreds of advertisers and thousands of subscribers on each campus. Conversion rates remained impressively high, with averages of 7 to 9 percent per promotion.

College Mobile Deals sounds a lot like Groupon, but there are crucial differences. Although the CMD affiliates did not run their own lists like Build-A-Bear, they *did* manage their own offers. Rather than splitting a percentage of their profits with College Mobile Deals, they paid CMD a set fee to be included in the outreach. As a result, the merchants could determine pricing that still kept their wares profitable.

The second major difference was that because of the immediacy of text messaging, companies could use the College Mobile Deals list to clear out excess inventory. Whereas Groupon clients have to wait for their offers to achieve a critical mass of users and "tip," CMD customers could send out coupons according to their daily inventories. Restaurants, for example, can only keep food around so long. Sending mobile coupons to a local audience of ravenous college students lets them clear out excess inventory and brings customers into the store where they're inclined to purchase other items such as beverages, sides, and desserts.

The third reason that College Mobile Deals worked so well was that local communities were reaching out to a local population of college students. Remember that Groupon writer who complained about trying to connect with "an audience we can't wrap our heads around"? Colleges are insular enough to pre-serve a communal feel on even the largest campuses. That sense of community counteracts some of the inherent disadvantages of a shared list. Students are more inclined to visit the local restaurants over and over, rather than branching out for an exploration of new horizons.

The College Mobile Deals business grew quickly before it was sold in 2009 to an integrated marketing company that wanted to reach that insular market—though not, however, for $6 billion.

Building Engagement to Increase Commerce

Mobile couponing is a precarious way to build lasting relation-ships. If done correctly, it can help drive more clients into your stores and build a list of interested and engaged consumers. If done wrong, it can alienate people and actually cost businesses money.

But you don't need to drive coupons or ask for donations to make mobile profitable. My experience has been that the most successful campaigns are the ones that focus on building rela-tionships first—and using those mobile relationships to feed into more traditional forms of commerce and fund-raising.

The Humane Society of the United States has been one of our most long-standing customers. They've built up a mobile list of 12,000 activists, primarily from sign-ups through online advocacy campaigns, such as ending the Canadian seal hunt and stopping puppy mills.

The Humane Society keeps its mobile list engaged with insider updates, breaking news alerts, and advocacy outreach. Indeed, it uses many of the tactics and strategies described throughout this book. For example, it sends local alerts around events, targeted to people's zip codes, to encourage community action. Its messages drive donations around topical events, like rescuing pets after Hurricane Irene. It even sends out weekly recipes for animal-free meals:

> HSUS Recipe of the Week: A delicious and unique soup featuring roasted red peppers! Romesco Soup Recipe: (http://m.humanesociety.org/recipes/romesco-soup.html). (ReplySTOP2OptOut)

There's no explicit appeal in a recipe for roasted red pepper soup. Telling users how to make "a delicious and unique" meal isn't asking supporters to show up at an event, lobby their senators, or donate more money. The mobile broadcast is simply providing a resource for the Humane Society's audience around their shared passion for animals.

Our research shows that that kind of openhanded engagement can have long-term financial benefit. When the Humane Society was doing year-end fund-raising in the cash-strapped winter of 2008, just as the economy was entering a steep downturn, it actually found that creating a text message connection with its constituents led to increased donations.

The Humane Society sent out an end-of-the-year text message to one segment of its list and left another segment of its list off the message. When the Society sent out an e-mail requesting year-end donations, it found that those people who had received the text message were 77 *percent more likely to donate.*

The Humane Society's results speak to a number of key beliefs about mobile outreach. First and foremost, spending the time and care to develop long-term relationships with your users can have a concrete financial impact. And secondly, a mobile campaign is just one element of a multiplatform communications campaign. Mobile cannot replace social media, TV advertising, e-mail outreach, on-the-ground events, or any other way that you connect with your members. It's just a powerful, immediate new way to further those relationships and to learn more about the people who matter the most to your organization.

The American Cancer Society Cancer Action Network (ACS CAN) is another organization that focuses on building up long-term engagement with its mobile list. ACS CAN is the advocacy wing of the American Cancer Society. It is dedicated to achieving policy changes that help the fight against cancer and advocates around issues such as smoke-free cities, increased cigarette taxes, and funding for cancer research through the National Institutes of Health. But ACS CAN understands that its members are not cold-blooded policy warriors. They're human beings, many of whom have been personally affected by cancer in their lives. As part of its efforts to engage with users, ACS CAN sent out a broadcast asking for some of those personal reminiscences:

> Have you celebrated a special milestone in your fight against cancer? Birthday, wedding, birth? Reply with your milestone now.

Hundreds of people responded to the message, and ACS CAN broadcast their responses on its website, http://www.acscan.org/celebratewithaction/milestones, to celebrate their accomplishments. Their stories ranged from the inspiring ("I'm going to college!") to the heartbreaking ("My sister died in my arms after a 4 yr. battle with breast cancer. Her 10 yr. old son witnessed her last breath! Protect kids from this.") The "milestones" campaign put a human face on the vital policy initiatives that ACS CAN fights for and reminded the ACS CAN membership of the importance of the cause.

However, ACS CAN was by no means acting cynically. It did not ask members to text in their personal stories in order to subliminally reinforce the importance of cancer advocacy. Rather, like their constituents, the members of ACS CAN are passionate about their cause. That's why they've made it their life's work. It is exactly that human connection to the cause of cancer that makes ACS CAN so effective.

In fact, it's that personal connection around any issue that drives engagement and leads to action. That's true whether the issue is a desire for policy change or a desire for a customized bear.

In an article in *Mobile Marketer*, Clive Maclean writes about the uses and abuses of mobile campaigns. Maclean is the CEO of Euro RSCG Discovery, the "Chicago-based North American data analytics, CRM and behavioral marketing agency network of Euro RSCG Worldwide." Euro RSCG Discovery focuses on creating "long-term customer relationships, rather than short-term acquisitions."[11] Maclean criticizes companies that "tak[e] what is a very personal medium and trea[t] it like push media," and argues that consumers "want to be engaged in a conversation."[12]

In the article, Maclean discusses a recent study of "prosumers"—that segment of the population that takes an active interest in the consumption decisions it makes—with a focus on the Millennial generation.[13] He notes that the study found that

> 77 percent of prosumers thought it was important to find brands that reflect their personality and 69 percent said it was important to find brands to which they could be loyal. . . . This generation desires a more personal approach to brand relationships. And they want them to fit seamlessly into their social worlds.

Maclean's point about prosumers seeking out "brands that reflect their personality" is a perfect epitome of the mobile campaigns discussed earlier. Organizations like ACS CAN and the Humane Society engage their users around a shared passion, not just a shared fund-raising goal. As a result, their members find that the brand embraces and in fact helps to define their personalities. Often, young "prosumers" and Millennials believe that the organizations to which they belong are not just reflections of their personality, but expressions of it.

In order to build those relationships, Maclean suggests a three-part strategy for SMS outreach that includes (1) offer-based texts, (2) engagement texts, and (3) brand news texts.

While "offer-based" texts and "brand news" are fairly straightforward, it's that second point, "engagement texts," that can be the most difficult to execute but also the most rewarding—both in terms of creative satisfaction and customer connection. Maclean elaborates:

> Engagement texts: A critical component of a successful mobile strategy, engagement texts go beyond offers, allowing the customer to participate.
>
> Examples include special partner offers that require no purchase, text to vote and added-value content. They are not promotional in any way and require no purchase to benefit. They enhance the overall brand experience.

ACS CAN asking its members for their cancer milestones is a perfect example of an "engagement" text. When the Alliance for Climate Education asked its users to text in their pledges, that was another example of engagement. You even could argue that the Humane Society's sending out a recipe is a way to "engage" its users in activities beyond the typical brand information.

Two Innovative Engagement Campaigns

The *New York Times* is one of the few newspapers to have both the innovative drive and the cultural resources to weather the transition to the new digital era. The *New York Times* has created an industry-leading web version of the paper, has built groundbreaking iPad extensions, and regularly produces online video that makes the digital *New York Times* experience much richer than a simple scan of the print newspaper.

Nevertheless, in a world of expanding news sources and shrinking ad budgets, the *New York Times* has to stay light on its feet in order to keep its place as the "newspaper of record" and center of the cultural conversation.

One clever way that the *New York Times* recently engaged its readership was by creating a mobile map around "Bird Week." Bird Week was a project of the *New York Times*'s City Room blog—"a salute to both the tourists and the birds who makes their homes here, featuring a gaggle of articles, graphics, photos, videos, maps and reader-participation opportunities."[14]

As a part of that gaggle, the *New York Times* worked with WNYC to create an "interactive map of bird-watching spots throughout the five boroughs."[15] They asked readers and listeners to text in their favorite haunts for birding and what types of birds they'd most recently seen. (Included were some pigeon sightings from outside Mobile Commons' Washington Street address.) The responses were collected into a Google map so that amateurs and aficionados alike could check out the new spots.

Avid ornithologists could also call in and regale an automated messaging machine with legends from their bird-watching exploits. The stories were added to the map as downloadable voice mails.

This book has previously discussed how mobile mapping can be a great tool for reportage; in Chapter 8, you'll see how governmental organizations are using it for disaster preparedness. The *New York Times* used a mobile map to create a quirky way to celebrate birding and connect with New Yorkers over an obscure cultural activity.

Like WNYC's "snow map," a mobile map suggests a new way that SMS can engage your audience, collate individual stories, and track trends. One person's story about local street conditions is an anecdote. A map full of these stories, however, takes on social and political implications.

Likewise, an individual's favorite spot to follow the swallow is just quaint. But a citywide repository of the best sites for birding could open up this hobby to thousands of new adventurers.

The Carnegie Museums' Summer Museum Adventure is another innovative use of mobile "engagement texts" to connect with users. Pittsburgh's Carnegie Museums are made up of the Carnegie Museum of Art, the Carnegie Museum of Natural History, the Carnegie Science Center, and the Andy Warhol Museum (henceforth collectively referred to as Carnegie). In the summer of 2011, Carnegie launched a new members-only Facebook page, and it wanted both to promote the page and to find a new way to engage its members.

Carnegie's solution was a "mobile scavenger hunt" that allowed even the most frequent museumgoers to discover new things about the museums. "Members, charge your cell phones!" the promotion ran:

> In celebration of the remaining days of summer—and to introduce the new Carnegie Museums Members Facebook page—we're inviting all members to participate in a Summer Museum Adventure. Just visit the four museums now 'til Labor Day, cell phone in hand, and participate in a mobile-phone scavenger hunt that will take you through the halls, galleries, and exhibition spaces.

Science buffs, art lovers, and dinosaur enthusiasts began their adventures by checking in at each museum and texting in a special start code to a designated number. Visitors then received multiple-choice questions that led them to discover some of the museums' hidden treasures.

There actually were rewards for getting the answers right. Savvy scavengers could win VIP tours of the exhibits or up to $500 in "Carnegie Cash." But the real winner was the museum, which found a new way to connect with its most loyal patrons and encourage membership among less frequent visitors.

The Future of Engagement

Those are just a few of the ways that mobile can be used as more than a quick one-off opportunity—and instead, as a way to connect with people, build enduring relationships, and ultimately to engage them around your brand's business or cause's concerns. But some futurists and innovative thinkers are exploring even more revolutionary new ways to interact with people through their cell phones.

"Gamification" has become an exciting topic for the kinds of big thinkers who regularly talk at TED and TEDX conferences. The basic idea is that by using the techniques and mechanics that make video games fun and addictive—points, badges, levels, and leaderboards—you can make everything from brushing your teeth each night to solving global problems both enjoyable and achievable.

Foursquare is one of the clearest examples of gamification. Members earn badges and "mayorships" based on exploring their cities and being loyal customers, respectively. Numerous other applications and enterprises are already adopting game techniques to both engage users and encourage repeat use.

In a talk at TEDX in Boston, Seth Priebatsch—"Chief Ninja" of SCVNGR, a mobile start-up dedicated to game mechanics—discussed the possibilities and perils of game dynamics. "The game layer is all about influence," he said. "It's about using dynamics, using forces, to influence the behavior of where you are, what you do there, how you do it."[16] That may sound sinister—but Priebatsch's point is that there's a tremendous opportunity here to do good. For example, in the last chapter, I discussed appointment reminders as one powerful way that healthcare organizations are using SMS. But Priebatsch speculates, what if people earned "points" if they showed up for those appointments after receiving those reminders? Might they not be even more incentivized? (That may sound a lot like a "nudge"—but, as I argued in the last chapter, a "nudge" is only morally thorny insofar as it's implemented without people's knowledge.)

Game designer Jane McGonigal thinks even bigger. In her book *Reality is Broken: Why Games Make Us Better and How They Can Change the World*, and at conference talks around the country, McGonigal argues that using game mechanics can actually make people happier, more productive, and more engaged with the world around them—and able to "solve problems like hunger, poverty, climate change, global conflict, [and] obesity."[17] In her talk at TED, she laid out her philosophy of game design: "We want to imagine the best case scenario outcome, and then we want to empower people to make that outcome a reality." For one example, McGonigal and her team made energy-efficient real-world living part of their game "World Without Oil." After the game was over, they tracked its participants, and discovered that a significant number of them adopted their eco-friendly game behaviors into their real lives.

What does this have to do with SMS? As Guy Krief, vice president of innovation at Upstream, argues in *Mobile Marketer*, mobile is the perfect medium for game mechanics, due to four of its qualities:

> The personal, intimate nature of a mobile device translates into higher potential impact/cut through.
>
> It is a time-sensitive device.
>
> Instant, easy interaction makes direct response much easier.
>
> Interactions can be tracked, leading to much greater accuracy in measurement.[18]

Krief in particular highlights the fact that because "consumers always carry their mobile device with them . . . mobile is the only marketing channel that enables a time component to be fully integrated in the gamification experience." He also speculates that because of mobile's ability to track interactions and segment outreach, gamification could become much more specific and therefore powerful. For example, rewards could be tailored to an individual's expressed interests. Or as Krief puts it, "whether the incentive is a free week of astrology or free week of sports scores could make a huge difference depending on who receives the offer."

While we may be a ways away from using game mechanics to end world hunger, we've already worked with customers to increase their user engagement through games. The Carnegie Museums' scavenger hunt, after all, was a game. Members were rewarded for their attentiveness to museum exhibits and their ability to answer multiple-choice questions.

As new types of socially beneficial games emerge, mobile is the perfect medium to form bonds and connect with users, and thereby provide gamers the power and the motivation to change the world.

7

USE DATA TO INCREASE CONVERSIONS BY STREAMLINING USERS' EXPERIENCE

Ben Stein, CTO and
Cofounder of Mobile
Commons

Imagine this scenario, which you have no doubt experienced: You call your bank for customer support. After navigating through a cumbersome phone tree, the automated system asks you to enter in your 16-digit account number. You scramble around in your personal effects for your wallet and painfully press the 16 keys. At last, you're transferred to a representative.

What's the first thing the customer service representative asks you? "Please tell me your 16-digit account number." Why didn't he know it already? Didn't you just key it in? Why can't their systems talk to one another?

Just a few years ago, that kind of technological inefficiency might have seemed acceptable. But as the digital world we live in becomes increasingly complex, we more and more expect the systems that surround us to work in seamless synchronization. And we're less and less likely to tolerate perceived inefficiencies. Whether you are trying to improve customer satisfaction, increase sales, or run a successful marketing campaign, getting the right message to the right person at the right time is critical.

That's particularly true when it comes to our mobile phones. Because people's mobile devices are so personal, they have very little patience for the convoluted interfaces or multiple-step signup processes that traditional web and e-mail marketing often use. That restriction, however, can be a blessing in disguise—just like having only 160 characters in a text message forces you to be concise in your outreach. By cutting through the noise and simplifying every possible step, you can eliminate drop-off and user fatigue, getting your users to complete your conversion.

This chapter will explain how to use data and databases to craft the correct message and get it to the users when they need it. In this context, message does not necessarily mean text message, as there are many other ways to communicate on a phone, including through the mobile web, apps, and of course phone calls. Furthermore, getting correct information to a user means both pushing out your message, such as a text message coupon or daily deal, and pulling information, such as mobile search.

Leverage the Union of Phone Systems with the Internet

One of the biggest changes of the Internet revolution is how many of our everyday services are now delivered via the Internet. People read books on Kindle that they purchase over wireless. Skype has enabled millions of people to cancel their landline. People watch television shows on Hulu and listen to streaming music with iTunes. Whether it's phone calls, books, music, or television, there's hardly a service that the Internet hasn't touched.

One of the best side effects of moving all this data and consumer behavior online is that all this information is now trackable, measurable, and actionable. Marketers can figure out in real time which books you're buying and recommend others you might like. Google knows which ads you've clicked on and tailors future ads accordingly.

Mobile has undergone a similar change. For 100 years, making a phone call involved connecting two physical circuits together. The phrase "long distance" literally meant that the wires had to travel a long distance across the country. That's why the phone companies could charge more, and in some cases a lot more, to make a long-distance call.

But when the next generation of phone systems were built, the wireless ones, they were done in a post-Internet world. The digital systems that make up our current wireless networks bear very little resemblance to the physical wires that Alexander Graham Bell strung up across the country. Suddenly, calling your friend across the country was no more expensive than calling your spouse in the next room.

As with every communication channel, these digital systems very quickly found themselves connected to the Internet, enabling an entirely new set of features to be built on top of them. The arcane and cryptic world of telecom technology slowly started becoming accessible to web developers. Sending text messages and making someone's phone ring became no more complicated than clicking a link on a web page. Once hackers and start-ups got their hands on this technology, they were able to transform this previously siloed communication into rich interactions with all the benefits of the Internet.

Suddenly, organizations could leverage this phenomenal channel in a smart and data-driven way.

Preload User Data to Increase Conversion and Decrease Drop-off

Marketers know that there is drop-off after every step you make a user go through. Add more fields to your web forms? Response rates fall off. Ask too many questions in a survey? Users won't finish it. There is a trade-off between asking for too much information and the response rate and completion rate.

Going back to the original example of the customer support system at the bank—given that the bank knows who is calling, what can it do to make the end user experience remarkable?

When users make a phone call, they leave you an excellent clue about who is calling: their phone number.

Number portability means that users can take their phone numbers with them when they change carriers. This has had an amazing side effect: people's cell phone numbers are an extremely accurate and durable identifier of who they are, second only to their social security number and maybe fingerprints. So when a user makes a phone call, you can suddenly add a huge amount of intelligence to what happens next.

Imagine that, instead of having to dial in your bank account number and then repeat it again for a sales representative, you have the following interaction. You call customer service and immediately hear a recording: "Hello. We see you are calling from 212-555-1234, which matches an account we have on file. Would you like help with that account?" You respond "Yes," and you are transferred to an agent who already has your account information pulled up in front of him or her.

Immediately, your entire experience of the customer service phone call has changed. And if you're on a call to make a purchase, you may be more inclined to actually move forward with the sale.

Use Data to Direct Users' Responses

One area in which this logic has had a tremendous impact is in political advocacy. Calling one's legislator to express a concern is fundamental to our democracy. But in reality, most citizens don't know who their representatives are or what their phone numbers are. Calling your legislator has tremendous value because he or she represents you and your interests. But calling the wrong legislator has little to no value.

The most common way to solve this problem is to have citizens call the Capitol Switchboard. Once they are connected, they can tell a live operator where they live, and the operator will connect the caller to his or her representative.

But if you know where your users live, because you have asked for their address or you have it in your CRM database already, you can easily find out their legislator by using their zip code. Then, when they make the phone call to support your cause, they can be automatically routed directly to *their* legislator, skipping the human intervention and the extra step of going through the switchboard, which would undoubtedly cause drop-off. Reform Immigration For America has had tremendous success with call-in campaigns that route people directly to their legislators.

When the funding of Teach for America (TFA) was in jeopardy, the organization found that a targeted call-in campaign mobilized congressional support. As a not-for-profit organization committed to educating children in low-income communities, Teach for America relies on federal funding. The group sends newly minted college graduates into communities across the country to help create a direct impact in the lives of children who might not otherwise have the same access to education. But without federal money, Teach for America could not continue to operate.

For 2011, TFA was requesting $50 million in federal funding so that it could reach one million students in low-income communities—and so that it could avoid cutting its existing staff. Representative Chris Van Hollen (D–MD) and Senator Barbara Mikulski (D–MD) had circulated letters of support to the Appropriations Committee, but TFA wanted to mobilize its base to generate additional congressional support.

TFA created two separate call-in campaigns—one targeted at the House, and one targeted at the Senate. TFA urged supporters to call their representatives and ask them to add their voices to Representative Van Hollen's and Senator Mikulski's efforts. The campaigns automatically routed callers to *their* representatives, making sure that the legislators were only called by their own constituents.

While the call-in campaign was just one leg of its outreach, TFA did see a direct—and almost proportional—correlation between how many phone calls a congressperson received and how likely he or she was to sign a letter of support. For example, only 8 percent of the representatives who received no calls signed the bill, compared to 29 percent of those who received 3 to 5 calls and 67 percent of those who received 11 or more calls. The results are a clear display of how constituent action can influence congressional decision making.

Call routing can be used for more than just congressional advocacy. It can also be a great tool for businesses. In an increasingly localized world, connecting a caller with a national chain in his or her local community is becoming an increasingly valuable proposition. Imagine calling a movie theater and being directly connected with your local chain for tickets and show times, *without* having to go through a long and painful phone tree. The same principle could apply to any number of similar businesses—restaurants, car rental agencies, and any company that operates on both national and local levels.

Just as phone tracking allows us to route a user to the most relevant number, it also lets an organization keep abreast of who is calling, and from where. Mobile Commons tracks every call that goes through our system. That information can be incredibly useful when you're trying to gauge the impact of your outreach or find out more about your most active customers or constituents.

Food & Water Watch has had tremendous success with its call-in campaigns. Not only do these campaigns generate enormous outpourings of support, but the organization is also able to use the information it gains to further segment and target its audience.

Food & Water Watch is a nonprofit organization dedicated to making sure the food we eat is clean, safe, and sustainable. Its "Ban Fracking" campaign is aimed at limiting a dangerous process called fracking that uses water and toxic chemicals to mine natural gas.

The Ban Fracking campaign has its heart and soul in telephone calls. To create the maximum political effect, Food & Water Watch organizes national call-in days to pressure the White House to pay attention to the fracking issue.

In order to best mobilize support, Food & Water Watch needed advanced call-in technology that would make it simple for its supporters to dial Washington. It also needed a system that was simple for the Food & Water Watch staff members to manage and track. "We used to rely on people self-reporting their calls to us," Meredith Begin of Food & Water Watch told us. "But we know that it's just a small percentage of people who actually do that."

First, Food & Water Watch reached out across all forms of media urging supporters to call the White House. To keep track of exactly where their calls were coming from, campaign planners set up five separate phone numbers: a number for their on-the-ground canvassers, a number in their e-mail outreach, a number for their click-to-call box on a Facebook page, a dedicated number for their coalition partners to use, and a number to include as part of a text broadcast to their mobile list.

Those people who clicked to call were asked if they wanted to opt-in to the broader Food & Water Watch mobile campaign. If they accepted, they received a follow-up text message asking them to pass the message on to three friends.

Each of the phone numbers given connected the callers directly to the White House. Additionally, the campaign used click-to-call to allow SMS, e-mail, and Facebook users to make the call instantly. That translated the impulse to help directly into action, with none of the intermediate steps that might lose a less determined caller.

Food & Water Watch created a steady stream of pressure by focusing its efforts not just at one moment, but in targeted waves throughout the course of the day. This ensured that the overloaded White House switchboard would be able to receive the maximum number of calls.

One recent Food & Water Watch call-in day yielded 6,000 calls to the White House—overwhelming the switchboard and creating a powerful political statement of voter support. After another call-in day, members of Food & Water Watch were invited to a White House meeting. There, they expressed the urgency of their mission—and hand-delivered a CD with hundreds of recorded voice mails that had *not* reached the White House switchboard. The White House representatives told them their call-in campaign had been "very effective"—the highest possible praise in advocacy.

Additionally, unlike with previous call-in campaigns, Food & Water Watch now knows exactly who are making calls, and when and where those calls come from. By using separate VoIP (voice over Internet protocol) numbers that allow telephone calls to be made over the Internet, it's easy for Food & Water Watch to tell what type of outreach is most effective—whether on the ground, Facebook, e-mail, or text.

Furthermore, because Food & Water Watch keeps a record of every click and call stored in every user's profile, it can determine who its most active advocates are. That means it can personalize its ongoing contact—to solicit more calls, to ask people to share actions with their friends, or just to say "thanks" for taking action. This data is not only helping the organization cement its relationships with current supporters—it's also giving planners ideas of where to look next in their ongoing campaign.

Connect with Users at the Right Time

Just as mobile can use data to connect a person to the right *place*, so it can also connect with them at the right *time*.

That's a crucial capability. A mobile phone is a person's most personal device. It's in his or her pocket or within arm's reach almost 24 hours a day. It's critical that if you are going to interrupt someone's day, you do so at a time when the person wants to hear from you.

For example, consider DoSomething.org, the organization that markets to teenagers, encouraging them to get out into the real world and volunteer. When sending text messages or triggering phone calls to teenagers, they will be very unhappy with you if you wake them up at seven o'clock in the morning. And if you call them in the middle of the day, they will be in school and won't get your message. As you would expect, the best time to reach teenagers is between 8 and 10 p.m.

Compare this with AARP, the largest membership organization in the United States, whose members are all 50 and older. AARP has an extremely active mobile list, routinely leveraging text messaging, phone calls, and the mobile web. With a completely different target demographic than Do Something, AARP can be very comfortable sending out its messages early in the morning or during the day, while a text message at 11 p.m. would probably be less welcome.

However it is important to remember that context is everything, and the right time is completely subjective. Consider a youth football camp run by Nike in summer 2010. Kids from all over the country attended a football camp with endorsements from famous NFL players. Training started at 7 a.m. each morning, which meant the kids all had to get up early—no small feat for a group of teenagers.

Nike created virtual alarm clocks to automatically call the teenagers early in the morning to wake them up. When they answered the phone, they were greeted with a recording of their favorite NFL player, such as Drew Brees, Hines Ward, Brian Urlacher, or Shawne Merriman. The players got the teenagers pumped up with their motivational wake-up calls. The phone calls came throughout the morning on a preset schedule as the kids had to be at different places in the training camp.

With mobile, more than any other medium in history, getting the message out at the right time is critical. If you get junk mail to your home address, it's annoying, but you just throw it out when you get home from work. Unwanted e-mail in your in-box, and you can just click the Spam button. But imagine getting woken up by a screaming football player at 6 a.m. on a Sunday morning. Unless you're a teenager at football camp, you are going to be incredibly unhappy. But for that targeted list of kids, getting the right message at the right time was incredibly effective.

Furthermore, the window when you can send an effective message over mobile is absurdly small compared to other communication channels. Direct mail delivery times are measured in days or even weeks. E-mail will be opened in hours or days, as people tend to read work e-mail during the day and personal e-mail in the evenings. But a wake-up call at 3 p.m. or a daily deal coupon delivered tomorrow is worthless.

In fact, unless the recipient is sleeping, one of the most exciting and useful aspects of text messaging is that the messages are read—most of them within 14 minutes. This is a very important statistic, because it means that the action, if it is going to be taken, will most likely happen within this time period. Because so many of these interactions such as web clicks, purchases, coupon redemption, and phone calls happen over the Internet, it is easy to track them and figure out when they happen.

Compare this to e-mail, where users may check their e-mail hours or even days later. When looking at a graph of user actions taken as a response to an e-mail blast, you see a small bump for the first few hours, a relatively flat curve that can last for a few days, and then a long tail lasting a week or more. When looking at the same graph of responses to a text message, the curve is completely different. You see a huge spike starting within seconds of the first text message going out that lasts between 10 minutes and 1 hour. After that, you see a precipitous drop-off with a long tail that barely lasts a day or two.

There are significant implications of the response rates and, more important, when they occur. For example, consider a text message that drives users to a live operator to buy tickets for a sporting event. Do you have enough operators to handle the sudden influx of calls? The worst possible scenario is having a willing buyer listen to your marketing message, call to place and order, and then be put on hold or get a busy signal because you lack the infrastructure to handle the inbound leads.

The most obvious solution to this problem when sending out text messages that you know will have a high response rate is to send them out slowly over the course of hours or even days. This will ensure a steady stream of phone calls rather than a huge up-front spike. Food & Water Watch sent out its messages over 30-minute increments to make sure as many people as possible actually reached the White House.

Interestingly, there are some situations where you actually *want* a huge spike of phone calls and can use text messaging to your advantage. For example, many "daily deals" companies create the illusion of scarcity and, with a limited inventory, make it difficult to "win" the desired item. The challenge of getting through is part of the marketing, and winning the item is a testament to that. Another case in which a spike of calls is desirable is rapid media response, where you want to overwhelm a TV or radio station with phone calls about a particular issue. In this scenario, clogging phone lines sends a strong message. But these cases are few and far between.

Also note that there is nothing unique to phone calls with respect to high spikes in volume. It happens that there is a human component to answering a phone call, which makes scaling them more difficult than scaling technology like a web server. The spikes can happen in the real world, too. For example, one of the most successful campaigns with the highest response rate is a mobile coupon campaign. Redeeming a coupon code online is easy enough to scale, but what if the code is redeemed in the store? If you send out 1,000 coupons for free ice cream on a college campus and 5 percent are redeemed, does your store have the capacity to service 50 simultaneous customers?

Use the Mobile Web Effectively

While usage of mobile web continues to skyrocket, it's very important to note that usage patterns and behavior on the mobile web differ from the desktop. Mobile is very well suited to following specific links and looking up particular information: following a link that someone posted on Twitter, looking up flight information, or reading a blog.

Mobile web is not very well suited to research and exploratory web surfing. When using a desktop browser, users have significantly more screen real estate—multiple tabs in a browser, for example, as well as easy access to take notes and send e-mails. And most important, users have a large physical keyboard on their desktop, which is missing on a mobile phone.

The combination of mobile web with text messaging is an incredibly effective way to disseminate information. Consider the strengths and weaknesses of each. Surfing and searching for information on the mobile web is hard, but it can be a rich environment that includes text, pictures, and video. Text messaging has a limited number of characters you can include in the body of the message, but its immediacy and targeted nature make it ideal for communicating.

By combining the two media, it is easy to send users information with an embedded link to learn more and get the full story. For example, Minnesota Public Radio (MPR) is a network of radio stations, operating over 34 regional stations. MPR sends weather updates via text message, as well as breaking news alerts. While the daily weather fits perfectly in 160 characters, the details of a breaking news alert do not. Therefore, when MPR sends a breaking news story, it will include a shortened web link that users can click through for more information. The most important step is to send users directly to the mobile web page containing the story they are interested in. The last place users want to end up when clicking a web link on their phone is your company's home page. Sending them to the exact right page, in this case a news story, provides the best end user experience on the phone: a seamless way to send a message to an interested and captive audience and then use the mobile web to get them exactly the information they want.

Another limitation of mobile browsers is the challenge of inputting data and filling out forms. Even with autocorrect and improved keyboards on iPhone and Android, even the simplest web forms can be daunting. Filling out a long, complex web form with a feature phone is close to impossible.

So given that user behavior on the mobile web is for very specific, targeted actions and that there is tremendous drop-off when users are confronted with data input, we can take steps to remediate these problems. Once again, we are going to use data and data-driven decisions to improve the end user experience and increase conversions.

From a technical perspective, determining the user's identity on a web page is a little harder than using the caller ID from a phone call. You don't get the browser's phone number information when visiting a web page, so you have to rely on other means. For example, if the user has visited your site from his or her phone before, you can and should leave a cookie. This will identify users when they return. A second technique is to send unique links to different users. If you know which link you sent each user, you can determine who users are when they click. This technique has been used for years by e-mail marketers, and it can easily be adopted in text messaging.

Once you know who a visitor is, you can tailor your content accordingly. Remember, on mobile the goal is to provide specific information first, with user freedom to surf and search being secondary. If users are going to a mobile page to look up their flight information and you know who they are, by default you should display their flight details. Don't make them type in their flight numbers.

Even more useful than dynamically changing content is using data to auto-populate form fields by using a CRM database and any information you already know about the user. For example, if users have given your company their name in the past, when they get to your form on a mobile page, you should have that field populated already.

By using data to automatically perform small steps, you streamline your users' interactive experience. You remove hurdles and make it that much easier for your target customers to do whatever it is you're asking them to do—whether that's sign a petition, donate money, or confirm their travel plans.

As an example, again consider AARP. AARP has a very sophisticated marketing organization and understands incredibly well how multiple steps can cause falloff in user activity. Therefore, it uses technology and data to significantly reduce the number of steps users need to go through when entering their payment information.

When AARP sends out text messages, all links are shortened and uniquely keyed to each user. When a user clicks on a link and is redirected to a landing page, AARP already knows who this person is. Therefore it can auto-populate the entire form with everything except the user's credit card number. Now, instead of 10 fields to fill out (first name, last name, address, city, state, etc.), the user only has to fill out a single field: the credit card number. By carefully considering the medium and the target audience, you can take these small steps to significantly increase conversions.

A note on security and privacy: be sure to hide any sensitive or private data. If you automatically fill in the user's credit card number on the form, and he or she then posts the link to Twitter, every user who visits that page will see that initial user's credit card information. It's critical not to auto-populate forms and web pages with information that will make the user feel like his or her trust has been violated.

Which data is acceptable to show, and which you should keep hidden, depends on your particular industry. For example, if you are providing a service related to healthcare, it would be unacceptable to show *any* personally identifiable information. Renewing a magazine subscription, on the other hand, may have looser requirements.

Of course, if the link is forwarded or a person changes addresses, there's always the chance that the wrong information could show up on a user's screen. That's why you should always include a clearly visible "Is this not you?" link. The user can then simply click the link and clear the data.

Use Data to Target Text Messages to Users' Specific Needs

As has been discussed throughout this book, sending out effective text messages requires a data-driven approach and analysis. You've already seen how to make sure that you're targeting the most relevant people with the most relevant information. But sometimes you want to specifically *exclude* someone who will be particularly uninterested in an offer or opportunity.

As discussed in Chapter 3, the Sacramento Kings have used its mobile list to increase ticket sales. In one example, it sent out mobile coupons for 15 percent off tickets if the user presented the text message at the ticket window. That created a tremendously successful promotion that spurred a race to the ticket window to redeem the coupons.

However, not everybody should be receiving a 15 percent discount on tickets. The Kings have to be extremely careful not to offer this promotion to one group in particular—its season ticket holders. The last thing highly valued season ticket holders want to get is an interruption on their phone trying to sell them something they don't need.

Using mobile data, the Kings can make sure that its offer excludes people for whom it's *not* relevant.

Using data can precisely target your message so that it only makes it into the hands of the people to whom it matters most. That targeting can extend to making sure it only reaches them at a *time* they need most. And by routing calls to their desired locations or prepopulating web forms, you can make sure your message reaches your target users in a *way* they need it most.

Combining those three, you can eliminate many of the inefficiencies of contemporary marketing and connect more directly with your audience.

8

ONE-TO-ONE
TRANSFORMS
WHOLE COMPANIES

In the depths of the dot-com bust, DoSomething.org seemed ready to close its doors. Starved for funding and reduced to one remaining full-time employee, the organization founded in 1993 by Michael Sanchez and Andrew Shue from television's *Melrose Place* could no longer afford to maintain its offices in cities across the country, where it trained teachers to go into the schools to foster volunteer projects that made a difference in their communities. But instead of folding, the organization decided to try something new: to communicate directly with the 13- to 25-year-olds it wanted to reach and restructure the company around their communication needs.

Do Something closed its satellite offices and began instead to build a digital campaign out of the media connections it already had. It built on its relationships with show business celebrities who appealed to young people. And it asked those celebrities to use their media platforms to talk about the organization—for example, the Jonas Brothers drew attention to Do Something in their concerts and television appearances, asking their audience to text in to learn about opportunities to volunteer. As young people made contact, Do Something began to discover where to reach them, what to offer them to motivate them to act, and how to make use of the super-users who wanted not just to volunteer now and then, but to launch their own campaigns for Do Something and even invent new ideas for future campaigns.

As news of the programs' successes spread, students from other parts of the country were inspired to get involved, and they could text in and find all the information they needed to start a club in their own school. Corporate sponsors got interested as well. Staples became part of a program to collect school supplies for disadvantaged students; Sprint sponsored a program called ThumbWars to prevent texting while driving. Do Something learned to build on its success by creating multiyear campaigns in which volunteers competed to outdo past accomplishments: in 2009, Teens for Jeans collected around 240,000 pair of jeans for teenagers in homeless shelters; in 2010 that number was 624,893.

The organization now works with 1,400 clubs around the country, yet all of them are supported by that one remaining office that survived the dot-com bust. Do Something is not just a mobile success story. It's an example of how overcoming the communications disconnect means a chance to streamline and restructure a company overall, preparing it to succeed in the digital age.

This chapter shows how this process can start with small steps that can be taken by even a single individual running an organization's communications—the person in charge of the mailing list, the e-mail list, and so forth. As a company becomes conversant in mobile tools and what they can do, mobile shifts from being a new kind of broadcast to true two-way communication, making it possible to listen, crowdsource new ideas, and empower members and customers to continue the organization's mission in ways that can grow enormously without requiring increases in staff.

Do Something's commitment to mobile emerged out of a new CEO's desire to find a sustainable way to engage young people. In a recent article, the *New York Times* documented how CEO Nancy Lublin transformed the charity from a brick-and-mortar operation into a center for online advocacy. In 2003, the article writes, "Do Something had just laid off 20 of its 21 staff members and had $75,000 in the bank. [Lublin] began closing offices around the country and replaced them with a Web site."[1]

Do Something succeeded by going where its target audience of teenagers was spending its time. In the early 2000s, that meant online. But a few years later, Do Something realized it needed to expand its reach. "We were already deep into web and social media engagement," said Stephanie Shih, digital strategist at Do Something.[2] "But we knew that teens loved to text. Most important, it was how they liked to talk to each other. Like so many of the awesome things we've done in the past, it was the brainchild of our CEO and Chief Old Person Nancy Lublin."

Do Something started using mobile as a way to provide local volunteer opportunities to young people in their neighborhoods—a program that is discussed in Chapter 4. Initially, it sent out its messages once a month, hooking in to volunteermatch.com and idealist.org to source the volunteer opportunities. Users received a message with a few ideas and could reply "more" to learn about others.

But the big aha moment for the company came when it realized that mobile messaging was more than just a new way to communicate with its already involved members. For one thing, it was an effective medium through which it could reengage lost members. As the *New York Times* describes it, the epiphany came when Lublin saw how effective mobile was at reengaging "defunct" teens:

> The staff had sent a simple text message to 500 teenagers—"Santa Cause says run a food drive in ur community 4 Tackle Hunger"—an annual food collection . . .
>
> The messages went to teenagers who were more or less "defunct," meaning that her organization, Do Something, had not heard from them in some time. For this appeal via text, some 20 percent returned to the fold in nine minutes. "It was nuts," Ms. Lublin said.

Since that time, Do Something has, according to Shih, "started to bake mobile engagement into every one of our campaigns and outreach tactics."

In one of its most recent initiatives, the organization created a text message scavenger hunt. Every day for 11 days, Do Something gave teams—or solo do-gooders, on the hunt by themselves—a new set of challenges focused on a new cause. Each challenge had its own point value, and teams could earn those points by sending in pictures of themselves completing the task. The team that got the most points won a ticket to Do

Something's Do Something Awards. There were a number of other prizes for the runners-up as well. And of course, every team was working toward the betterment of their local communities.

Do Something used mobile engagement to turn local activism into a fun, community-driven event. In the process, it also built up interest in its annual awards in its engaged audience of young people. And because the challenges were across a variety of causes, it exposed young people to new issues and ways that they could help out.

In another recent campaign, on the tenth anniversary of September 11, 2001, Do Something launched "Decade of Thanks"—an online, interactive collection of messages dedicated to the emergency workers who risked their lives that day. Users could log on to the website or text in their messages of thanks, and the messages were plotted on a map in a powerful symbol of nationwide gratitude.

And on November 11, 2011, Do Something launched an anti-bullying campaign. "We're giving away $$ + popcorn for ppl who take action against bullying," one text message read. "To be eligible, step up to a bully + share your story w/us via txt. Yep, it's that easy."

Do Something incentivizes its audience not just with money or prizes (like delicious popcorn), but also with the opportunity to share. The Facebook generation considers sharing their exploits and adventures as one of the chief appeals of any action they take. By using text messaging to give its audience a voice, Do Something makes taking a stand more relevant and more enticing.

It also makes it more universally applicable. "We've been able to reach people we wouldn't normally have been able to reach," said Shih. "While not all kids have access to the Internet at home, 75 percent of all teenagers have their own cell phone. We can't beat those numbers. Teens text their friends more than they even hang out with them in real life."

One reason why Do Something has been so successful with its mobile efforts is its commitment to data. As discussed throughout this book, data can be vital in refining an organization's message—and new digital media open up a wealth of new metrics. Do Something has put that philosophy into action. The organization was recently featured by nonprofit blogger Beth Kanter under the headline "How Can Nonprofits Switch to a Data-Driven Culture?"[3]

"[They] are leaders in the nonprofit world for exhibiting the characteristics and work habits of a data-driven organization," Kanter writes. She notes that the Do Something board is composed of tech leaders, like LinkedIn's Reid Hoffman and Snapfish's Raj Kapoor. And she points out that CEO Nancy Lublin hired a data analyst, Bob Philbin:

> Bob . . . believes that part of the problem is moving away from making decisions by "gut" feelings, or intuition. Bob says, "The data should tell us whether or not the program is effective."

But while Do Something has achieved banner results through data, the heart of its success has come from never forgetting the human element of its outreach. It makes sure its audience knows that there's a live person on the other end of the text. "The level of interaction [through mobile] is much more intimate—not in a creepy way," Shih says. "Our users have really loved realizing there's a real, live human on the other hand of this short code when they assumed it was just a bot."

Shih cited one example of an initiative that Do Something actually *declined*. The White House asked them to partner on a mobile app to help fight teen dating abuse. Shih explained:

> I'm sorry, but that is just not realistic. The barriers to getting a potential abusee to download this app are just too high—who wants THAT icon on their main iPhone page? How often are the future victims going to be able to anticipate the abuse? How many victims consider themselves "domestic violence victims"? The list goes on. Needless to say, we didn't get involved.
>
> I think as we move onward and upward with all this shiny, sleek, new technology, the value of "real" interaction (that is, with a real person, albeit digitally) is going to become very important.

Do Something came to mobile for two reasons—one, because it was a cost-effective way to do its outreach. And two, because that was where its audience was spending their time. Mobile was never just another technological novelty to be used for its own sake. Instead, Do Something looked to mobile engagement as a vehicle for improved *human* communication. As a result, it has transformed its organization—and is able to set itself lofty new goals. "The goal is to use mobile technology to sign up 3.8 million members by 2014," the *New York Times* reports. That's a long way from one community office.

How WNYC Came to Mobile

Like Do Something, public radio station WNYC came to mobile organically. While trying to reach its audience of New Yorkers, it realized that the most direct way to get feedback was through mobile messaging.

WNYC has had a long and storied history of innovation. The station is one of the oldest radio stations in the United States, first broadcasting on July 8, 1924, using "a second-hand transmitter shipped from Brazil."[4] According to *Wikipedia*, "with the commencement of WNYC's operations, the City of New York became one of the first American municipalities to be directly involved in broadcasting." In 1929, WNYC broadcast *Masterwork Hour*, radio's first program of recorded classical music. On December 7, 1941, it was the first American radio station to report the Japanese attack on Pearl Harbor.

The station's spirit of innovation has extended into the way it has explored and embraced digital media. We've already mentioned how the channel's innovative "snow map" fact-checked Mayor Bloomberg's claims about the street cleanup and how WNYC partnered with the *New York Times* to create the bird map, the directory of the best birding spots in the city.

But, as with Do Something, WNYC didn't embrace mobile through an organizational directive. It came to mobile through a few staff members' experimental desire to find new ways to connect with listeners.

In 2007, the station's then-producer, Jim Colgan, had just come across the new buzzword "crowdsourcing" while working on the *Brian Lehrer Show*. The show was devoted to interacting with its audience of New York listeners. But it only had seven phone lines. As Colgan describes it, "At any one time we had all these topics on the show which resonated with a lot of New Yorkers. The show has a very strong foothold in the life and culture of New York. But the only way we could allow people to contribute was through these seven phone lines."[5]

Colgan and his colleagues wanted to use new media to find ways to further engage their listeners—and "crowdsource" some reportage in local New York communities. At the time, there was "a lot of talk of sustainability in the city. The Mayor was coming up with his 30-year sustainability plan. So we decided on a project that would ask people to help us find out how many SUVs were in the city as a percentage of all cars. New Yorkers pride themselves on their environmental awareness, so we thought it would be interesting to see how New Yorkers actually live," Colgan said.

The show asked listeners to perform a simple task. They should walk outside their door, count the number of cars on their block, and count how many of them were gas-guzzling SUVs. They were then to go back to the show's website and report their findings. At the time, WNYC did not have a simple way for its staff to take people's reports and assemble them into structured data, so it asked the audience to put their results in the website's Comments section. Colgan then went through the comments and manually copy-and-pasted them into an Excel spreadsheet, before plotting the points on a map.

This wasn't a scientific study. In fact, that was part of the appeal. A Harris poll might have been reported as news, if it was reported at all. But rather than merely talking on-air about data from a study or a survey, the SUV report could relate the actual experiences of the city's inhabitants and the show's listeners. "Everybody was interested in it—even those people who didn't participate," said Colgan.

The station decided the initiative was successful enough to try another crowdsourcing project. The show decided to look into the disparity in prices for household goods at different grocery stores throughout the city. So, it asked listeners to go out to their local bodegas or groceries and do a price check on a standard bill of goods: a quart of nonorganic regular whole milk, a head of iceberg lettuce ("none of your fancy arugula," said Colgan), and a six-pack of Budweiser bottles—three items station staff members felt would be widely available.

Once again, people went out into their neighborhoods and reported their results in the Comments section on the website, and once again Colgan had to manually import the findings into Excel. But the result was another interesting story about price differentials throughout the city.

The show was surprised, however, when staff members called some of the stores in question to do fact-checking on the prices. The store owners and managers were often defensive and evasive. They wanted to know who was calling, why they were asking, what it was about. WNYC realized that there was no way a reporter or a producer could have gone into these grocery stores and repeated the experiment—they would have been met with suspicion and obstruction. Only through crowdsourcing the task to citizen journalists was the station able to report on the subject.

Still, there was one big drawback—and that was the effort required to convert people's reports into a usable format. "The whole time I kept thinking—if only people could do this on their cell phones while they were in the store or on their block," said Colgan. "That would come in as structured data. That was part of the impetus for us to get an SMS provider."

Two years later, the station had one. This was around the time of the 2010 Democratic primary in New York. In the days before the election, WNYC asked people to text in the word "POLL" to 30644 to get a reminder to vote on Election Day.

But the station also wanted to use the opportunity of the election to crowdsource another news story. New York had just adopted a new ballot, with a new design and a new technology—optical scan. So WNYC asked people to report on the new ballot booths and ballot forms. This time, however, it asked people to text in. That gave the reportage an immediacy that it would not have had if the station needed to rely on people to head home, remember to navigate to its website, and remember to key in their experiences. "Starting from 6 a.m. when the polls opened, people were texting us when they voted," said Colgan. "As a result, at WNYC, we were one of the first people to report on that issue. Because we had that tie-in with our listeners, we were one of the first to report that story."

WNYC also heard something the staff had not been expecting. People were having concerns about their privacy. The new voting booths didn't have curtains, and voters felt like they could be monitored. That on-the-ground feedback became a news story for the reporters as well.

Those early steps into mobile have led WNYC to engage with its audiences in even more significant ways. The "snow map" has already been discussed in Chapter 3. When the snowstorm of December 2010 caught New York by surprise, the station plotted stories from people around the city about the street cleanup in their neighborhoods. The map provided an opportunity to crowdsource information—and fact-checked the mayor on his claims about the city's cleanup effort.

"My experience with the early crowdsourcing experiments made me realize the power of just mapping something," said Colgan. "It allows people to see all the results, in a very intuitive way. You can the results that are related to you and where you live."

The WNYC "snow map" also fed on-air programming for the station. "We got really good stories about how people were not able to get to the hospital, not able to feed their pets," said Colgan. "We gave people the opportunity to send us an audio message, which generated an MP3 that we could connect with the data. So when reporters couldn't go out and interview people, we were able to actually crowdsource the tape-gathering job. We had all this great tape from listeners that we could just insert into the newscasts."

Colgan was particularly pleased with how quickly the station could create a mobile campaign. Without having to set up an onerous reporting structure, it could both learn and disseminate the stories of people throughout the city—"almost as an afterthought," he said.

The "snow map" was a groundbreaking use of mobile in news, and it recently won an Online Journalism Award from the Online News Association. It also galvanized people throughout the station. Like Do Something's Tackle Hunger food drive campaign, the "snow map" may have been the aha moment that made WNYC fully realize how mobile messaging could speak to its target users in an entirely new way. According to Colgan,

> Internally, people realized the power of engaging with the listeners with a story like that, and its potential of generating leads for reporters to follow up on, and as a way to generate breaking news . . . that was fast and efficient and generated structured data.

Since the "snow map," WNYC has continued to explore and innovate with mobile. On the news morning show *The Takeaway*, the station wanted to get stories from listeners about how high gas prices were affecting them. It told its audience to text in "What was the most recent price you got at the pump," and asked them about their changing habits—if they had changed their vacation plans, for example. As with the "snow map," WNYC was able to generate audio stories and once again turn the data into a map.

"It was great for our radio station. It was great for our website. It was a great way to connect with our listeners—and a great way for them to share their stories and be heard," Colgan said. "When it's just a one-way conversation with media, you don't relate to the information in the same way as you do when someone like you has played a role in it."

Subsequently, WNYC has crowdsourced reports about cell phone access in the New York City subway system. The station worked with the *New York Times* to create the bird map. It recently started working with the *New York Times* again on a new program called SchoolBook. SchoolBook is a microsite dedicated to providing a holistic overview of New York City's schools and creating "resources that educators, experts, policymakers, parents and taxpayers can add to and draw from."[6] According to the project's website,

> We will tell you how schools do on tests, where classrooms are most crowded, who has the highest-paid teachers and what we know about the demographics of the student body.[7]

While SchoolBook pulls in many resources from multiple data sources, the planners also wanted to get information from the concerned parents and stakeholders themselves. To that end, the project is asking parents, teachers, students, administrators, and any other citizens to text in "SCHOOLS" to 30644. Once a month, respondents will be asked for their insights and opinions.

Additionally, as discussed in the next chapter, when Hurricane Irene was approaching New York, WNYC worked on a few different projects that linked mobile messaging and mapping and created a valuable resource for emergency preparedness.

The station is also finding ways to use mobile to connect with audiences at events. For example, WNYC recently hosted an event about the controversial policy of stop-and-frisk, through which police are allowed to pat down people whom they might find suspicious. At the event, the moderators asked people in the room whether or not they had been stopped and frisked, and if they had subsequently been arrested. People texted in their responses, and WNYC displayed the results of the poll using a graph in the room.

Additionally, WNYC has started to explore new ways for mobile to help the station connect with its audience around the cultural life of the city. For one simple example, it recently helped get out concert information at the city's Celebrate Brooklyn festival. Celebrate Brooklyn is a summer-long concert series in which multiple big-name acts perform. (If you haven't heard of The Decemberists, Animal Collective, Sufjan Stevens, or Bon Iver—well, they're big names in Brooklyn.)

But while many people were aware of the series generally, they might not remember to log in to the series' website to see who was playing on which nights. "One common complaint is that you hear about a great band that played—only after they played," said Colgan. "We wanted to give people the chance to catch them." WNYC let people text in to sign up for a mobile list to get alerts in advance of which bands were playing.

And the station is continuing to innovate. "Right now, WNYC is trying to find a way for residents of New York to have their voices heard in the political process," said Colgan. Have they ever contacted a council member? Did they feel like their voice was heard? And how did that relate to their voting decisions?

WNYC's mobile project began because Jim Colgan and a few of his peers had "crowdsourcing" on their minds and wanted to see how they could make it happen. And because they needed a convenient way to connect with New Yorkers with minimal effort and staff resources. From a limited-technology project in which the station asked people to peer at the cars outside their door, WNYC is now engaging its listeners about the questions at the very heart of their democracy. "Mobile has changed our whole approach to how we can tap into the power of our audience," said Colgan. Now stations in California, Florida, and elsewhere, across many different media, are looking to follow the station's lead.

The Human Rights Campaign Goes Mobile

The Human Rights Campaign (HRC) came to mobile in a slightly different way than WNYC or Do Something. Realizing that mobile was an innovative way to connect with its tech-savvy constituents, the campaign fostered a creative push across many media to build up its mobile list; it then inspired that list to take concrete action. But, like Do Something, WNYC, and all the organizations discussed throughout this book, HRC has consistently pushed at the boundaries of how to use mobile to create a human connection.

HRC is the largest Lesbian, Gay, Bisexual, and Transgender (LGBT) advocacy group and lobby organization. Members divide their time between advocating politically for the rights of the LGBT community and helping that community through educational and outreach programs.[8] Mobile, they realized, provided an opportunity both to channel political action and to foster the human connection across a digital medium.

At the DMA 2009 Washington Nonprofit Conference, Dane Grams, then HRC's online strategy director, laid out what HRC's projects have been and the benefit the organization has seen.

> We decided to branch into this . . . mostly because I think our users on our file are tech savvy. It was an opportunity for us to pioneer this area. . . . We can utilize rapid-

response technology. If we have an action going into Congress, it's a way to get phone calls immediately. We can go out to a critical mass of supporters on a moment's notice. It's part of a new communications channel. And it really for us is laying the groundwork for tomorrow's fund-raising. E-mail rates continue to decline. Response rates continue to decline. I think there's a lot to be said for investing in mobile now.

HRC started out by cross promoting its mobile campaign across all of its outreach channels, including its website, its press releases, in its magazine, and its e-mail outreach. "It became part of everything we did," Grams said. "Every action that we do, every donation page we have, we ask for someone's mobile. We ask them to opt into our mobile marketing program. And they're doing it in droves."

Early on, HRC used its mobile list to keep its audience informed about LGBT issues that mattered to them. "When the California Supreme Court came down on gay marriage in California, we sent out a text message to our folks," Grams said. "We reminded people to watch Obama's acceptance speech in Denver." HRC also used its mobile campaign to break organizational news. When Joe Biden announced he would be the keynote speaker at the HRC National Dinner, the campaign announced this to its mobile list. It sold tickets to events, cultivated donors, and sent out holiday greetings. "It's another way to remind folks that you're thinking about them," Grams said.

HRC has also used its mobile list to drive its audience to take political action. As discussed in the last chapter, a mobile campaign can have the technology to automatically route people's calls to their local legislators. HRC has used that power to drive thousands of calls to Congress around hot-button issues that mattered to its constituents. For example, in the recent battle over marriage equality in New York, HRC targeted specific legislators with phone calls from their constituents who overwhelmingly supported the issue.

HRC has also routed calls to Cabinet officials and the State Department—for example, trying to pressure the State Department to back a UN Resolution. It has launched mobile-only petitions, giving its members the opportunity to have their voices heard in opposition to John McCain, for example, or in support of Barack Obama. Upward of 17 percent of its mobile list signs up for those petitions. And, like WNYC and many others, it has used mobile alerts to remind people to get out the vote.

But HRC has really innovated in creating mobile "products" that hold politicians and companies responsible for their opinions on LGBT issues. As one example, it created a "Shopper's Guide" that let people text in to find out how friendly stores are to LGBT issues.

HRC ranks Fortune 1000 companies on its "practices and policies for LGBT Americans." But it's often hard for people to remember which companies are friendly to the causes they care about—especially when they're out for a day of shopping. So HRC created a mobile database that allows people to learn about companies' LGBT inclusiveness policies via text message. Users simply text in the word "SHOP" and then the name of a company to receive a text message rating that company's LGBT friendliness.

HRC's program allows consumers concerned with companies' LGBT policies to get specific information about those companies anytime, anywhere. Most important, it allows users to get that information right when they're considering making a purchase—at a store, while browsing the web, or even when they're making investment choices.

HRC also created a similar database program for politicians. As Grams describes it, "This past October and November [2008], you could query your member of Congress by texting the word VOTE and their name, and we would spit back their particular ranking in congress to your phone so you knew where they stood on our issues."

Additionally, HRC uses its mobile list to foster a digital LGBT community and celebrate the milestones that mean the most to its constituents. It has hosted moments of silence on the anniversary of the death of Matthew Shepard, a gay teenager who was murdered in a horrific hate crime. And in the recent celebrations over the passage of New York's marriage equality bill, HRC helped its constituents across the country sound off digitally. After the final vote was in, HRC sent a text message to supporters across the country, asking them to text in their celebration messages. Then, using the same mapping technology that WNYC has popularized, the group plotted those messages digitally, creating a visual record of the nation-wide celebration.

Like many of our partners, HRC has found that increased engagement actually leads to increased fund-raising. "People on this program are more likely to give money to the organization," Grams said. As of Grams's presentation in 2009:

- Over 33 percent of the organization's mobile subscribers had donated to HRC at some point (33.2 percent).

- Seventeen percent had donated since joining the list.

- And almost 6 percent gave their first gift to the organization only after joining the mobile action network.

Mobile even allowed HRC to see which subscribers were the most likely to give. For example, 50 percent of people who used the keyword "EQUAL" had given since joining, whereas 33 percent of people who used the keyword "HRC" have given since joining.

Grams concluded his talk by noting, "This *is* having influence on people and their giving habits."

By building mobile into every part of the organization's outreach and by using digital means to foster a very human spirit of activism and community, HRC has seen massive growth in its list. In September 2007, HRC's mobile list had 5,000 subscribers. One and a half years later, it had 30,000. As of October 2011, HRC had over 90,000 subscribers to its mobile list, a committed group of advocates who believe in the organization's cause and take action on its issues.

Nike Just Texts It

Sportswear giant Nike has been one of the most innovative companies across all spheres of digital engagement. To cite just a few projects from its incredibly extensive library of digital creations:

The Nike ID website lets people customize their own shoes. The Nike+ partnership with Apple builds a digital sensor right into the shoe so that runners can track their distance, their performance, and their route. In 2007, as part of a microsite for Nike Air, it created an online "visual symphony" to give people the experience of running or playing sports in its shoes.[9] The "Nike Shout" campaign was a "social installation" in Asia that let soccer fans use Facebook and Twitter to broadcast messages of support onto huge LED displays running the length of the field during games.[10]

"I think customization and integrated digital technology will become what people expect," Nike CEO Mark Parker told the German magazine *032C*. "So we are committed to being at the forefront of both of those areas."[11]

Knowing that mission, it should come as no surprise that Nike is also at the forefront of innovating across mobile—especially given how much text messaging is a part of young people's lives. For Nike, mobile is not a way to sell more products or direct people to its stores. Rather, it's an opportunity to find new and creative ways to support the passion for sports and build the ongoing relationships in a lifestyle brand. "We're now communicating much more surgically with individual communities alongside our broader communications that go out to the world," Parker said.

We recently worked with Nike on one such "surgical" communications strategy—engaging teen athletes at the Penn Relays. The Penn Relays bring more than 22,000 athletes to Philadelphia each year to compete in the nation's premiere high school and college track event—with over 100,000 spectators cheering them on.

Nike wanted to connect with the teens attending the relays and establish a central destination for their experience of the event. To engage the thousands of people at the event, Nike provided race updates, exclusive interviews, free shwag, and much more. Inside the stadium, the Nike Cheer Zone gave out free T-shirts and cowbells to help the crowd go wild. And in the Nike tent, attendees could find free laces, tune-ups for their running spikes, live feeds from the track, a sports desk with athlete interviews, and a beauty shop for hair braiding—or a buzz cut of the Nike swoosh. With all this and more, Nike gave event attendees numerous new ways to have fun and enjoy the relays.

The challenge was letting people know about it. The Penn Relays average one race every five minutes, providing plenty to do and even more to see. To become a focal point for teens attending the event, Nike created a mobile campaign to get the word out. After all, if there's one thing that can grab a teen's attention no matter what else is going on, it's text messaging.

That's especially true when the texts provide useful information and access to free stuff. Nike deployed a multipart strategy that got teens interested in the Nike activities before the meet even started. It publicized its mobile short code throughout the web and at numerous live events across the country. Teens were told to text in "SPIKE" to 69866 to be "in the know" about all of Nike's activities—or to text in "DARK" to 69866 to find the next location of the Nike ice cream truck (see Figure 8.1). The call to action went out in a variety of ways:

- Facebook fan pages

- Banner ads on runnerspace.com before and during the relays

- A prominently placed chalkboard at the events

- An ad on the outside of the Nike ice cream truck

- Foldout Z-cards handed out at the relays

Figure 8.1 **The Nike ice cream truck invited teen athletes to join the Nike list well in advance of the relay.** (*Ross Dettman for Nike.*)

- High school visits made by the Nike Mobile Van in the months leading up to the Penn Relays

By engaging its target audience well in advance of the actual event, Nike ensured that come race day, it would immediately be able to get the word out about all of the Nike-sponsored activities.

Then, on the day of the relays, Nike sent out messages that provided something for everyone, from the casual spectator to the most hard-core relay-o-phile. It sent out news about time-sensitive events, such as when star athletes would be interviewed at the Nike sports desk. It scheduled flash "Cheer Zone" cheering meet ups. And it let its mobile list know about special offers, such as free Volt green laces or VIP wristbands.

The Penn Relays are for teens who love a race—and they proved it by literally running to the Nike tent. When Nike sent out a blast promising the first 20 visitors a free VIP wristband, there was an instant overflow to the booth, which created a sense of excitement about the Nike tent that continued over the course of the relays.

"What better way is there to keep in touch with high schoolers throughout Penn Relays weekend than via text message!" said Jen Blank, Nike's account manager at the marketing firm MKTG. "I think kids used more energy running to our tent when a text came through than in their races!"

By texting their messages to a screen or being invited to cheer for their favorite team, teens came to feel that Nike was helping their voices be heard. It's that kind of brand loyalty that inspires brand fans to get the company logo buzzed into their haircut! The steady stream of traffic to the booth, coupled with the carefully timed text messages, ensured that Nike was on the minds of spectators and athletes from the first starting gun to the last lap. Best of all, Nike built a list of devoted race fans it can reach out to in the future.

No longer just a sneaker company, Nike is becoming a lifetime sports clearinghouse, nurturing a long-term conversation that leads to decades of sales of sports equipment and related purchases—all discovered and facilitated by the relationship with the Nike brand.

Building New Connections and Changing the Way We Communicate

Getting started with mobile is simple and painless. It can emerge naturally from a quest to find new ways to connect with an old audience. Or it can be part of a calculated attempt to take advantage of a new technological medium. But in every case, mobile helps organizations build new connections and enhance existing relationships.

This chapter has discussed just a few of the ways that companies and nonprofits have internalized those opportunities and created human connections. Of course, this is just a brief overview of a few organizations—by no means is this list comprehensive. Many other organizations are as committed to mobile, from Reform Immigration For America to AARP.

In the following chapter, we'll discuss ways in which mobile is not just transforming companies but actually changing the way societies and citizens can communicate.

9

ONE-TO-ONE TRANSFORMS COMMUNICATIONS FOR EVERYONE

Mobile is fast becoming not just the most popular way to send a message, but the number one way people access the Internet. According to the work of Mary Meeker at Morgan Stanley, in the United States the mobile web will become larger than the desktop web by 2013—and already it is the only meaningful connection that underserved populations use to participate in the digital world. Yet among both phone users and Internet providers, this demographic shift is not well understood. Even as mobile phones become ubiquitous, many people simply conflate mobile communications with an iPhone app, or assume that the Internet service they're receiving on their laptop is the same as the one that reaches their Droid. To succeed with integrated mobile strategies in the long term, you will need to understand the bigger revolution underway.

When you set aside received wisdom and look at what people are actually doing with their phones, you can see that mobile has progressed far beyond one-off marketing curios. It's even evolved beyond simply being the best way that friends and family members keep in touch. It's much more than a way to schedule a meet-up or find a nearby sushi bar. Mobile has become a way to get information you need about healthcare and housing. It's a way to keep in touch with governments during a disaster. It can find the closest bus. For many people, a mobile phone is a convenient and affordable substitute for a computer. Mobile will soon be a necessary tool for anyone trying to be a fully engaged member of society, as essential as the newspaper, the landline telephone, or the television were in their heydays— the tether that connects everyone to everything.

Yet mobile carriers such as Verizon and major players such as Google still insist that unlike these other crucial communications channels, mobile communications should not be regulated by the government. The carriers want to restrict for themselves the power to determine what content can and cannot travel across their networks. No attention is paid to the fact that the mobile devices used by the poorest people are often not able to receive the messages they need. Parents could be unable to receive information about postnatal care or about their children's schools. It is likely that the carriers are not even aware of the existence of such services, nor of the ways their own policies cause hardship and exclude significant numbers of people from the revolutionary opportunities described in this book. They often view mobile as a mere novelty marketing channel that is not in need of protection. And so, despite widespread agreement that a digital connection is essential for meaningful civic participation, there is now a movement to leave mobile at the mercy of carrier interests that are, at best, in the dark about the critical tool it has become.

This chapter puts examples of mobile use for healthcare, politics, education, economic opportunity, and community engagement in a larger context to show how integrated mobile campaigns are essential not only for organizations to succeed, but also for democratic countries to realize our shared commitment to an informed and engaged citizenry.

One-to-One Transforms Health Information

Chapter 5 explored ways in which healthcare mobile messaging can inspire people to take action and encourage healthier lifestyles. It discussed how healthcare providers are taking advantage of the immediacy of mobile messaging to help people stop smoking, remember their medications, resist their cravings, confirm their appointments, and much more.

But mobile messaging's power to inspire action is just *one* way in which it's revolutionizing the healthcare industry. Healthcare providers are also using mobile to communicate knowledge, provide immediate information, and foster a human connection. And in the process, they're revolutionizing the way our society communicates.

During the H1N1 flu scare in 2009, for example, the California Department of Public Health had a database of all the places where Californians could get vaccinations against the virus. The problem was, it had no simple way for people to access that information.

The department created a mobile database that let people text in to find not just a complete list of clinics—but to find the clinic closest to them. People texted in their address and immediately received the closest H1N1 vaccination facility, including an address, a phone number, and hours of operation. (The technology behind this program is the same that the Human Rights Campaign uses to let people text in and find out how politicians and stores fare on LGBT issues.)

A week after texting in to find a vaccine, people were sent a message asking if they indeed got vaccinated at the location suggested. If they responded "no," they were asked why not. Over 50 percent of the people who were surveyed responded to the text. Thirty-three percent of the respondents confirmed they got a flu shot at the recommended location. As to why respondents did not get the shot, 40 percent said they would get the shot later and 17 percent had been vaccinated elsewhere.

Those are incredible response rates. "Getting a flu shot" is one of those nebulous tasks that people know is good for them, but for which they're often not willing to disturb their routine. That's especially true for an unfamiliar threat like H1N1, which people may read about in the papers or hear about on the news, but with which we have no real contact in our daily lives. The California Department of Public Health transformed the somewhat abstract "get a flu shot" to "get a flu shot in your neighborhood, right now." It turned healthy behavior into a convenient and achievable daily task that citizens could take.

The California Department of Public Health's H1N1 campaign represents just one way that organizations are using mobile to communicate lifesaving information to the public. The California Poison Control System sends out informational text broadcasts every week, in Spanish and English, about poison-related issues, such as toy recalls and antifreeze dangers.

Harvard Pilgrim Healthcare created an innovative program for the parents of young children that combines informational messaging with behavior tracking. The campaign sends out educational text messages—for example, informing parents about the sugar content of juices and energy drinks or the importance of exercise. It has combined that information with related tracking questions, asking parents how many sugary beverages their children drank that week, how much television they watched, how many hours they played outside, and so on. As soon as the parents respond, they're automatically sent follow-up messages—either praising them for their parenting skills, or encouraging them to do better in the future.

The system also tracks week to week whether the users are making improvements in their parenting. So, for example, if in week one the parents let their children watch 40 hours of television, but in week two they only let them watch 30 hours, the system would register that improvement—while still encouraging them to do better. Throughout the program, the parents occasionally meet with a counselor to evaluate their progress.

Centene, a managed healthcare provider, has created a similar campaign that combines informational messaging with behavior tracking—in this case, targeted at expecting and new mothers for prenatal and postnatal care. Expecting mothers sign up in their doctor's office and give their due date. Then, as with *Martha Stewart Weddings'* campaign targeted at brides around their wedding dates, the mothers receive text messages with health information timed around when the baby is due. Once the child is born, the mothers start to receive information relevant to the postnatal care, such as the importance of regular health checkups. Mothers also can opt in to take an informational tracking survey. If they agree, every week the mothers receive a message asking about their breastfeeding habits and weight. Women are incentivized to sign up for the program through credits in their Centene account.

By sending vital health knowledge right to people's pockets, these programs democratize healthcare information and make it easy for people to stay informed. The Harvard Pilgrim and Centene campaigns also suggest another usage for mobile communications—keeping track of medical behaviors. It can be hard for researchers to gather accurate data about which actions people are actually taking. Text messages, because they are so targeted and so immediate, make it simple for people to provide researchers that vital information. When the Harvard Pilgrim study texts a parent asking how many hours his or her child has spent watching television, it's a simple thing to respond "30." There are no complicated forms to fill out—respondents just answer the questions and hit send. That not only provides valuable information in the aggregate; it also provides opportunities for medical professionals to help out specific individuals who may be unwittingly setting themselves up for health problems down the line.

A number of teen-focused organizations are experimenting with new ways to use the personal relationship that mobile communication can foster to connect young people with sexual health information. Sexual health information is uniquely difficult to communicate. Teens are often misinformed, and the web is full of rumors and half-truths. Furthermore, given the high sensitivity of sexual health issues, young people may not feel comfortable asking their teachers, their parents, or the doctors who have treated their families for generations. Thus, they often have no real recourse for firsthand, accurate information. Even a clinic visit or a voice-to-voice phone hotline might seem too personal.

A few innovative healthcare groups are trying to solve that problem by creating mobile campaigns that communicate directly with teens, in real time, over text message. The Planned Parenthood Federation of America (PPFA) lets teens text in their sexual health questions and receive an immediate response from a health educator via live chat over SMS. Spots on MTV and banners on the PPFA mobile site direct teens seeking support to text the organization with questions, which are answered by trained professionals who point to information and, in some cases, can book the teens for an appointment at their local clinic—all via text.

The Iowa Department of Public Health runs a similar program called TxtTina. Like Planned Parenthood's initiative, TxtTina gives teens direct access to health educators, who respond in real time. The Alexandria Office of Women also lets teens text in their health-related questions; they receive a text message back within 24 hours.

Text messaging provides these teens with an anonymous direct link with a real person who can dispel myths and provide factual information on some of the most pressing questions they face—about delaying sex, birth control, STD prevention and treatment, emergency contraception, sexual orientation, pregnancy testing, and more.

Behavior tracking, informational messaging, and direct communications are just a few of the ways that medical groups are exploring this new medium. Almost every week, we see a new innovative use of mobile messaging in the healthcare field. And as new data continues to reinforce the effectiveness of mobile campaigns, more and more organizations are likely to explore this frontier.

One-to-One Transforms Government

The California Department of Public Health's initiative hints at another way that mobile messaging is transforming society: by providing a conduit for government agencies to communicate with citizens. Like healthcare organizations, governments often have vital information they need to get into people's hands. But until the rise of mobile phones, there was never a reliable way to do so.

Cities and states around the country, along with the federal government itself, are already exploring how to use new digital media to better communicate with their populations. In 2009, President Obama appointed Aneesh Chopra as the nation's first chief technology officer (CTO). His job, in the president's words, is to "promote technological innovation to help the country meet its goals such as job creation, reducing health care costs, and protecting the homeland."[1] Chopra works in concert with Vivek Kundra, the country's chief information officer (CIO). State and city governments are also employing CTOs, CIOs, and CDOs (chief digital officers). (If there weren't a wealth of acronyms, it wouldn't be government.) Their job is to understand the implications of emerging technology and harness the new platforms for more effective governance.

In New York—as in other places—the city is exploring how best to use digital technology to engage its citizens. In an article in O'Reilly Radar, Alex Howard writes, "New York City has become the epicenter for many experiments in governance, from citizensourcing smarter government to participatory budgeting to embracing a broader future as a data platform."[2] Those experiments include everything from Web 1.0 (maintaining NYC.gov as a hub of governmental news) to Web 2.0 (pushing city updates to the Twitter feed) and beyond.

The "beyond" includes opening up the city's wealth of data to outside developers in a way that can encourage innovation and foster the development of groundbreaking new applications. The article quotes Rachel Sterne, New York's chief digital officer, on the way in which New York wants to mimic the successes of major corporations in opening up *their* platforms. Sterne says,

> How can New York City, with the enormous amount of data and resources we have, think of itself the same way Facebook has an API ecosystem or Twitter does? This can enable us to produce a more user-centric experience of government. It democratizes the exchange of information and services.

Sterne goes on to express how the city's disaster preparedness around Hurricane Irene created a test case for the opening up of city data to outside developers. Last August, as it looked like a category two hurricane would hit New York City head-on, Mayor Bloomberg ordered rigorous preparedness measures to ensure that everybody was safe—including closing city bridges to traffic and mandatory evacuations of the city's coastal regions.

As New Yorkers prepared for the unexpected storm, people were unsure if they were part of the evacuation zone and didn't know what measures they should take to stay safe. The city *had* a map of where the evacuation zones were, but not many people knew about it. In response, organizations developed resources that used the city's information, but then innovated on top of it to make it more accessible. As the Radar article elaborates:

> The key insight coming out of that August weekend, with respect to the city acting as a platform during unprecedented demands for information, was that the open data that NYC provided on evacuation zones was used by other organizations to build maps. When NYC.gov buckled under heavy traffic, the city government turned to the Internet to share important resources. "As long as the right information was getting to citizens, that's all that matters," said Sterne.

In the article, Sterne also mentions our customer WNYC, which was one of the leaders in developing applications to disseminate information about the hurricane. In one example, the station created a mobile application that let New Yorkers text in their addresses to find out which flood zone they were in. If they were in Zone A, along the city's coastal regions, they would know to evacuate. If they were in Zone B, they knew to prepare themselves and stock up on supplies and essentials. And if they were in one of the other zones, they knew that they could breathe easy.

While many groups created online maps that plotted the flood zones, WNYC's text messaging program circumvented the steps where people would have to go to a computer, log in, and check themselves on a map. The mobile messages opened up the information to those New Yorkers who might not have easy access to a computer or the Internet. And rather than having to decipher a sometimes confusing map, it gave the definitive answer about which zone a user was in.

WNYC and the *New York Times* also partnered to create a crowdsourced map that let New Yorkers text in signs of the city being prepared or unprepared. People could submit their observations and leave a voice message; all the submissions were plotted on a map for anyone to read or hear. For example, one message read, "Over 50 conEd vehicles parked in union square." (On the other hand, one user, safe in the interior of Brooklyn, texted in, "We're all going to the neighborhood bar, all have umbrellas.")

The New York Office of Emergency Management also released a crowdmap, this one powered by the open-source software company Ushahidi, that let people report storm damages. By texting in "IRENE" to 877877, anyone could submit reports of things like power outages, downed trees, unsecured construction material, or flooding.

New York City actually ended up being largely spared by Hurricane Irene. The storm barely touched down in the city, instead saving the brunt of its devastation for other areas in the region. (The flooding in Pennsylvania "reached levels that had not been seen in that city in more than 140 years.")[3] Some people speculated that the mayor's reaction was actually overcompensation for the *lack* of city preparedness during the previous winter's blizzard—when streets were clogged with snow and WNYC created its "snow map."[4]

But the extent of disaster preparedness showed how new technology could help the city in the face of a real catastrophe. Reliable information, sent straight to residents' mobile phone, could save lives in the event of a real emergency—especially when power outages might temporarily take televisions, computers, and Internet routers offline. Having a map of citywide damage is more than just a technological gewgaw. It can be a valuable aid to city officials seeking to help citizens, repair damage, and secure streets.

New Types of Transportation Information

Transit authorities are another group experimenting extensively with mobile. There are very few ways to reach commuters; by definition, they're on the move. So if you're trying to help people get reliable information during their commute to work, mobile messaging isn't just the best option—it may be the only option. Both the New York and the San Francisco MTAs are using new technology to get transit information to commuters that can help simplify commutes, decrease traffic congestion, and improve their cities' quality of life.

San Francisco is developing a revolutionary parking system that can provide commuters up-to-date information on where to find the closest parking spot. It's called SFpark and, among its other capabilities (for one—there's an iPhone app), it lets San Franciscans text in to easily find parking spaces near them. People text in "GARAGE" and their address or intersection to 877877, and they're sent back a list of nearby garages and their codes. They then text in which garage they want, and SFpark sends the location, hours, and rates—as well as how many spaces are currently available. Ed Reiskin, executive director of the San Francisco MTA, was quoted in the *San Francisco Chronicle* on the program's merits:

> These programs will not only provide enhanced conven-
> ience and less congestion and pollution associated with
> one's search for parking, but also allows us to optimize the
> use of our parking facilities.[5]

By centralizing and disseminating parking information over mobile, SFpark makes it that much easier to find a spot. That may sound like a trivial convenience if you live somewhere without bad traffic. But providing accurate, up-to-date parking information can unclog congested streets and save valuable commute time. It's also green. Finding a spot without all the driving around saves not just time, but gas and fuel emissions, too.

In New York, the MTA is developing a program that provides commuters real-time information about the location of the nearest bus through the Internet, the mobile web, and both smartphone and text messaging technology. Users can text in the bus stop or the intersection where they are and receive back information about how far away the closest bus is—allowing them to gauge their commutes. With reliable information about bus times easily accessible, commuters are more likely to use buses—decreasing traffic congestion and increasing the efficient use of public utilities. And, by providing people a better experience of transit in general, the MTA's program hopes to increase the citywide quality of life.

Both the New York and the San Francisco programs are revolutionizing the way people live their lives. No longer will commuters be subject to the guesswork of circling between lots or wondering anxiously at a bus stop if they should just take a cab. Through mobile technology, they can find accurate answers, wherever they are, whenever they need the information. The world is filled with data; governments are now finding creative ways to get it into the hands of people who need it most.

Mobile Housing Information

"Sending vital information to the people who need it most" might well be the motto of a mobile messaging program from the Capital Area Foreclosure Network (CAFN). CAFN helps at-risk residents within the Washington Metropolitan Area (Washington, D.C., and its suburbs in Maryland and Northern Virginia) who are facing foreclosure—and, just as problematic, are in danger of being lured in by foreclosure rescue scams.

With decreasing house prices and increasing unemployment in the Washington region, many homeowners are having difficulty paying their mortgages. According to CAFN's press release, "Data from March 2011 shows that more than 9 percent of all loans (approximately 115,000 mortgages) in the

Washington, D.C., metropolitan area were in foreclosure or delinquent."[6] Homeowners facing foreclosure are often also confronted with a barrage of confusing and misleading information—often from scam artists looking to profit from their dire financial situation. Chuck Bean of the Nonprofit Roundtable of Greater Washington, who coleads CAFN, describes it: "So many individuals who have lost their homes have fallen victim twice: first to predatory lenders and then to foreclosure rescue scam artists who promise they can save people's homes, charge thousands of dollars, and do nothing to help."

CAFN wanted to connect people in need with the experts who could help them. And they wanted to provide "advice, reminders, and alerts" that could keep homeowners informed about their options and free from the dangers of scams. So they launched a bilingual mobile messaging campaign to get the information to the people in the at-risk communities who need it. As its press release describes the program:

> Parties can opt-in to the service by using their mobile device to text HOME or CASA to 877-877, and will then immediately receive critical information and a hotline number to use when they are ready to connect to a counselor at a HUD approved counseling organization. After that, subscribers will receive periodic reminders, information about foreclosure prevention programs available in their jurisdiction, such as the new mediation programs in D.C. and Maryland, follow-up instructions, alerts to scams, financial literacy tips, and much more.[7]

Using a bilingual mobile campaign, CAFN can reach the at-risk populations it might not be able to get ahold of otherwise. The press release cites a May 2010 Pew Report, which reported that "87% of Hispanic households have multiple mobile phones and use them more than any other personal or handheld technology."

As Peggy Sand, director of the regional coalition, said, "Mobile phones are the most effective, easy and affordable way to connect with struggling residents."

Other Uses of Mobile in Government

Those are just a few of the ways that governments are using mobile messaging to transform communications with their citizens. And there are many, many more programs, across all facets of society.

The New York City Department of Education recently asked parents to apply for an open seat on a citywide or community education council. Parents were told to text "APPLY" to 877877 to get more information, to learn about the schools in their district, and to get involved on behalf of their children.

And, in one more mundane example, the residents of one area of England are being asked to use text messaging to turn in scofflaw pet owners. People are requested to send a text message report if they see pet owners not cleaning up after their pets.[8] According to an article about the new law:

Stockport Council recently launched a new text message alert system to crack down on irresponsible dog owners.

The new system allows residents who witness dog owners failing to clear up their pets foul to report the incident via a text message directly to the Council's Dog Warden Service.

The following information is requested in the text:

- Specific date and time of the fouling
- Specific location of the fouling
- Brief description of dog and the owner
- The name of the person texting (if he or she is willing to provide this)

Reporting on scofflaw pet owners is hardly as inspiring a use for mobile messaging as communicating vital healthcare information where it's needed most. And indeed, the Dog Warden Service's initiative has more than a hint of the classic English nanny state. But it's an experiment, and it shows the way in which communities are exploring new ways to use technology to enforce their laws and interact with their governments.

From healthcare to disaster preparedness to transit to pet fouling—from the routine to the silly—mobile messaging is transforming the way we communicate with our elected officials and the way we interact with society.

The Battle for Free Airwaves

Yet, in spite of the multiple ways that governments are using mobile, they have not yet extended their regulatory power into the mobile sphere. Superficially, that may sound ideal. After all, who wants government bureaucracy screwing up the pristine new technological frontiers? But in government's place, mobile providers such as Verizon and AT&T police themselves and make their own rules. And they have adopted policies that restrict and control what information people are able to access.

In *The Master Switch*, Tim Wu discusses how Western Union, the first telecommunications monopoly, picked and chose whose telegrams it was going to carry. That allowed the company to exclusively circulate news reports from its ideological ally the Associated Press. With only one nationwide news service, and only one nationwide telegraph system to disseminate the news, Western Union and the AP were able to effectively control national opinion. They even crowned their own president, Rutherford B. Hayes, who was nothing more than "an obscure Ohio politician" before the AP's information campaign.[9] When AT&T's telephones displaced Western Union's telegraphs, AT&T was able to avoid government regulation by promising to carry any and all content, without discrimination—a policy called common carriage. Wu explains the significance:

> Despite being a monopoly, Bell was committing itself to noninterference and making itself equally open to all users of its service. . . . This is the essence of common carriage, a concept that may seem esoteric, but is as fundamental to free communications over wires and frequencies as the First Amendment is to free expression. . . .

Bell's dedication to common carriage was a promise
to serve any customer willing to pay, charge fixed rates,
and carry his or her traffic without discrimination.

By committing to common carriage, AT&T agreed that
anybody could make a phone call and it would be carried over the
same phone lines in the same way. That may seem trivial to people today. However, over the past decade, as carriers have
sought to control and regulate the information that crosses
their networks, they're challenging that same very basic
telecommunications premise in a battle over "net neutrality."
As Wu explains the argument in an essay in *Slate*, the basic
premise of the Internet gives people the freedom to "vote with
their clicks"—to choose whether they prefer Instapundit to
cnn.com or the search engine A9 to Google. Wu writes,

> Is it a problem, then, if the gatekeepers of the Internet (in
> most places, a duopoly of the local phone and cable com-
> panies) discriminate between favored and disfavored uses
> of the Internet? To take a strong example, would it be a
> problem if AT&T makes it slower and harder to reach
> Gmail and quicker and easier to reach Yahoo! mail?[10]

Internet providers want to be able to control which information crosses their networks—and even the speed at which it
crosses them. Some carriers want to charge premium fees in
exchange for faster service. They argue that they laid the cables
and built the towers, so they should have the right to monetize

them as they see fit. Otherwise, why would they continue to build communications infrastructure?

The problem is—if some companies are getting faster service, then that means that everybody else is getting slower service. So those sites and organizations that are too small or too poor to afford the premium fees will get left behind in favor of those companies that have more resources or that develop better relationships with the carriers. And those groups that the carriers don't want on their networks at all could basically be cut off from reaching the public.

As Wu explains, that could be a disaster for innovation. World-revolutionizing sites like Facebook, Amazon, and Google started as small services that built up a loyal—and then a global—user base. Without free access to people's attention, could technological innovation happen at the same rate? And think how much more true that is for opinion sites like Talking Points Memo or the Huffington Post. If CNN is informing you faster than MSNBC is—in this era of instant gratification, you may choose CNN, even if you marginally prefer the quality of MSNBC's content.

So far, net neutrality has largely been the status quo for the "wireline" Internet—the kind of Internet you use at your desktop or laptop computer. The problem is that those rules do not apply to *mobile* communications—the networks you access through your mobile phone. That means that the wireless providers can effectively control what content will or won't be sent over their service. As an article on the Save the Internet Coalition's website describes it,

If AT&T or Verizon wants to make a particular news site or social networking site load slower on your iPhone or Android, they can do that. If they want to block mobile apps like Facebook or Netflix, they can do that too.[11]

As phones become just small computers, and more and more people use their mobile devices as their primary way of connecting with their peers and accessing the online universe, those powers becomes more problematic. That's especially true since this isn't just a fanciful bugbear of corporate malfeasance. We've already seen examples where the carriers have exercised their power.

In 2007, Verizon blocked a text message communications program from the abortion rights group Naral Pro-Choice America. The campaign was similar to many of the campaigns I've described in this book, consisting of text messages to the organization's supporters that encouraged political advocacy. For example, one text read:

> End Bush's global gag rule against birth control for world's poorest women! Call Congress. (202) 224-3121. Thnx! Naral Text4Choice."[12]

Most of the leading wireless carriers agreed to carry Naral's text messages. But Verizon refused, claiming it had the right "to block 'controversial or unsavory' text messages."

The problem is—it does have that right. Because there's limited government regulation over mobile communications, carriers have extensive power to determine what gets across their lines. That's true even though Naral was only sending the message to people who had already opted in to its campaign—people who, effectively, had *requested* it. As Naral's president, Nancy Keenan, told the *New York Times*,

> No company should be allowed to censor the message we want to send to people who have asked us to send it to them. . . . Regardless of people's political views, Verizon customers should decide what action to take on their phones. Why does Verizon get to make that choice for them?"[13]

In late 2010, the FCC adopted Open Internet rules in an attempt to establish some clarity to Internet regulation. But as Wu writes in the TechCrunch blog, the FCC's ruling is incredibly vague, and basically hedges on many of the most important questions in the net neutrality debate.[14] By keeping its rulings unclear, Wu argues, the FCC effectively reinforces the status quo. He writes, "The uncertainty supports a continued openness on the wired internet, while also sanctioning a wireless internet that is semi-closed and dominated by commercial content." While the wireline Internet can be a "happier home" for innovation, the wireless Internet will be under carrier control and "favor old-school commercial content." (Wu also argues that in addition to the carriers, the makers of the actual devices have tremendous regulatory power. For example, Apple curates the app store to decide which applications to allow and which to forbid.)

Just as rapid innovation is coming to mobile communications, the carriers' policies and the FCC's vagaries threaten to stifle it. Eric Schmidt, in his keynote at Salesforce's Dreamforce conference, predicted that "the next Mark Zuckerberg" will be someone who combines "local, mobile, and social." But what if that person's technology is deprived of the oxygen it needs to grow because of restrictive policies or arbitrary decisions?

Part of the disconnect between mobile innovators and mobile carriers is that carriers view mobile marketing as an inconsequential novelty. They remember mobile marketing as it existed several years ago and don't have a real awareness of the vast amount of innovation that has taken place, as exemplified by the companies and campaigns discussed throughout this book. Basically, the zeitgeist within carriers has not caught up with the highly innovative reality outside. They have a hard time distinguishing the ringtone scams of a decade ago with Nike's outreach to teen athletes or Harvard Pilgrim's health information campaign.

The problem is that the entirety of enterprise mobile communications as we've described it is just a blip on the carriers' radar—miniscule compared to their core business. The vast majority of carrier business is selling mobile phones as a service to people who communicate with other people. Even Mobile Commons' biggest program is tiny in comparison to that daily business. As significant as mobile campaigns are to the people whose lives they touch—they're small compared to the total traffic of the carriers.

Because mobile marketers are not central to the carriers' revenue streams, we're met with a lot of bureaucratic red tape when we try to engage with them in dialogue. Companies, governments, healthcare groups, and nonprofits are developing innovative campaigns that combine text, voice, and the mobile web—but they're regulated in the same way as the daily horoscope. Imagine looking down at a city from an airplane thousands of feet in the sky; it's impossible to tell the skyscrapers from the grass huts.

I believe that many of the problems we're facing could be solved through more carrier openness about their practices and an ongoing dialogue with carriers at a high level about what's permissible within the mobile realm. Right now, our programs exist at the mercy of the carriers, without any regulation. Short of comprehensive government intervention, the carriers need to offer clarity about their decision-making processes.

By adopting fair and transparent regulations, the carriers can provide people the services they desire, they can encourage innovation—and at the same time, they can still earn a healthy profit. In his *Slate* piece, Wu writes, "I believe that it's better to have consumers pay more for service than to have AT&T picking and choosing winners on the network."[15]

Nobody's arguing for free access to the Internet, or for anything that would jeopardize the carriers' expensive investments in their infrastructure. Rather, people want to pay for service that's fair, that fosters the spirit of invention, and that allows the development of the digital content that makes the carriers necessary. By keeping mobile channels open to everybody, the carriers can create an environment where innovation thrives, and all types of organizations and institutions can experiment freely.

In 1985, Friedhelm Hillebrand invented the text message—an obscure paging system for businesspeople with car phones. Just over a quarter century later, that humble innovation has revolutionized the world we live in. Now citizens of all economic status have immediate access to the information they need—whether that's information about how to catch the most convenient bus, what pills they should be taking, or how to stay safe in times of crisis. By making it simple and convenient for organizations and people to communicate, text messaging is reshaping our society.

CONCLUSION

In the preceding chapters, we showed how businesses and organizations are able to use mobile to transform their preexisting communication channels. These channels range from old-fashioned print, broadcast ads, and live events to the social web. This transformation enables genuine and effective ongoing conversations that make media a true partner rather than an intermediary controlled by others.

The benefit of being able to engage in that conversation creates a sea change. You are now able to listen to the individual customer in real time and respond instantly.

The key to creating this type of engagement is to look at the all the places you touch your audience—packaging, ads, the web, live events, and press. Each point of contact is a potential starting point for the **one-to-one conversation**. You must always ask, "What compelling call to action can I make in order to engage the potential customer or supporter?"

Mobile is a particularly effective method of beginning the conversation. Everyone has a mobile phone with him or her at all times, and you can be up and running very quickly at very low cost. The goal, however, is to have your media channels working together. Your website, e-mail, social media channels, television ads, press, and live events can all be coordinated.

The previous chapters show how to use existing communications to begin the **one-to-one conversation** with tangible results. As your campaign evolves, you can then add additional channels to find out even more about your target users. More important, you will be able to listen to all of these channels in one single place. As customer relations management (CRM) tools such as Salesforce.com become simpler to use and more accessible, creating such profiles will become easier. Regardless of the channel, the principle remains the same—bring people into your database and foster a direct relationship rather than relying on third parties as an intermediary.

Additionally, as the mobile web overtakes the rest of the web, it is important to understand how mobile web behavior differs and benefits from the **one-to-one conversation**. Mobile web users need to be sent to the exact right page based on their profile. People do not want to surf or fill out web forms on mobile devices. By utilizing data-rich user profiles and text messaging, you can send people directly to mobile web pages that are auto-populated with account information, such as medical histories or travel itineraries. Businesses and organizations that are doing this find desired outcomes to be significantly greater and less expensive to achieve.

We hope this book has been helpful in getting the conversation going. Thank you for reading it.

NOTES

Introduction

1. http://www.nytimes.com/2009/09/24/business/smallbusiness/24texting .html?pagewanted=all.

Chapter 1

1. http://latimesblogs.latimes.com/technology/2009/05/invented-text -messaging.html.
2. http://en.wikipedia.org/wiki/SMS.
3. http://www.pcworld.com/article/191887/why_is_email_spam_so_much_ worse_than_sms_spam.html.
4. Tim Wu. *The Master Switch: The Rise and Fall of Information Empires* (New York: Alfred A Knopf, 2010).
5. Thomas Friedman, *The World is Flat*, p. 248.
6. Ken Auletta, *The Highway Men*, (San Diego: Harvest Books/Harcourt, Brace and Company, 1998).
7. https://www.salesforce.com/crm/sales-force-automation/.
8. http://media.mit.edu/ventures/EPROM/whyafrica.html.
9. http://www.newyorker.com/online/blogs/newsdesk/2011/03/africa-cell -phone-revolution.html#ixzz1Uxv4rNQa.
10. http://www.csmonitor.com/World/Making-a-difference/Change-Agent/ 2011/0705/Cell-phone-banking-could-lift-Africa-s-farmers.
11. http://www.csmonitor.com/World/Making-a-difference/Change-Agent/ 2011/0705/Cell-phone-banking-could-lift-Africa-s-farmers.
12. http://www.youtube.com/watch?feature=player_embedded&v=sdD9AP mouzo.

Chapter 2

1. Larry Weintraub, "6 experimental social media campaigns," *iMediaConnection*, April 19, 2010.
2. Taddy Hall, "10 Essential Rules for Brands in Social Media," *Ad Age*, March 22, 2010.
3. http://www.youtube.com/watch?v=JDl5hb0XbfY.
4. http://latimesblogs.latimes.com/technology/2009/03/skittles-twitte.html.
5. http://smartblogs.com/socialmedia/2011/02/11/live-from-social-media -week-the-suxorz-picks-the-worst-social-media-moves-of-2010/.
6. http://www.slideshare.net/edlee/ddb-social-media-survey.

7. http://www.dmnews.com/retailers-continue-to-invest-in-mobile-and-social-despite-poor-roi/article/201960/.

8. http://mashable.com/2010/02/22/dennys-twitter/.

9. http://news.cnet.com/GM-slow-to-react-to-nasty-ads/2100-1024_3-6057143.html?tag=newsmap#ixzz1X29L9sn7.

10. http://www.newyorker.com/reporting/2010/10/04/101004fa_fact_gladwell #ixzz1WvzHUsuz.

11. Ibid.

12. http://www.nybooks.com/articles/archives/2011/apr/07/internet-better-or-worse/?page=1#fn-1.

13. http://edition.cnn.com/2011/TECH/innovation/02/21/egypt.internet .revolution/index.html.

14. http://www.nybooks.com/articles/archives/2011/apr/07/internet-better-or-worse/?page=1#fn-1.

15. http://www.nytimes.com/2011/02/14/world/middleeast/14egypt-tunisia -protests.html?_r=3.

Chapter 3

1. http://news.yahoo.com/us-newspaper-ad-revenue-falls-another-7-pct -223048125.html.

2. http://en.wikipedia.org/wiki/This_American_Life.

3. http://mobileactive.org/american-life-joins-mobile-giving-revolution.

Chapter 4

1. http://www.youtube.com/watch?v=JDl5hb0XbfY.

2. *Reform Immigration With Your Cell Phone*, Reform Immigration For America.

Chapter 5

1. http://news.softpedia.com/news/Reminder-SMS-Messages-Make-More -Young-People-Vote-65547.shtml.

2. http://pewinternet.org/Reports/2011/Cell-Phone-Texting-2011.aspx.

3. http://techcrunch.com/2011/02/07/comscore-says-you-dont-got-mail -web-email-usage-declines-59-among-teens/.

4. Mark Zuckerberg, Speech at Facebook Event, San Francisco, CA, November 15, 2010.

5. http://www.pediatricsupersite.com/view.aspx?rid=82061.

6. Amy Dockser Marcus, "The Real Drug Problem: Forgetting to Take Them—As Many as Half of Patients Fail to Follow Their Regimen; a Pillbox That Can Nag," *Wall Street Journal*, October 21, 2003. http://www .aegis.com/news/wsj/2003/WJ031006.html.

7. http://www.thelancet.com/journals/lancet/article/PIIS0140-6736%2810% 2961997-6/abstract.

8. http://www.nytimes.com/2009/11/05/health/05chen.html.

9. *New York City Department of Health and Mental Hygiene's Text Messaging Randomized Control Trial*.

10. http://mobihealthnews.com/10393/studies-sms-effective-for-smoking -cessation/.

11. Heather Cole-Lewis and Trace Kershaw, "Text Messaging as a Toll for Behavior Change in Disease Prevention and Management," *Epidemiologic Reviews* 32 (2010): 56–69.
12. http://www.newyorker.com/arts/critics/books/2008/02/25/080225crbo_books_kolbert?currentPage=all.
13. http://www.nytimes.com/2008/03/16/books/review/Berreby-t.html.
14. http://www.newyorker.com/arts/critics/books/2008/02/25/080225crbo_books_kolbert#ixzz1Zfxm1KR8.
15. http://en.wikipedia.org/wiki/Predictably_Irrational.
16. http://www.nytimes.com/2008/03/16/books/review/Berreby-t.html.
17. Dan Ariely, *Predictably Irrational:The Hidden Forces That Shape Our Decisions*, (New York: HarperCollins, 2008).
18. Amy Dockser Marcus, "The Real Drug Problem: Forgetting to Take Them—As Many as Half of Patients Fail to Follow Their Regimen; a Pillbox That Can Nag," *Wall Street Journal*, October 21, 2003. http://www.aegis.com/news/wsj/2003/WJ031006.html.
19. Heather Cole-Lewis and Trace Kershaw, "Text Messaging as a Toll for Behavior Change in Disease Prevention and Management," *Epidemiologic Reviews* 32 (2010): 56–69.
20. Richard H. Thaler and Cass R. Sunstein, *Nudge: Improving Decisions About Health, Wealth, and Happiness* (New Haven, CT: Yale University Press, 2008).
21. http://www.youtube.com/watch?v=DD-fUJs5t_k&feature= related.

Chapter 6

1. http://en.wikipedia.org/wiki/Groupon.
2. http://online.wsj.com/article_email/SB10001424052748704828104576021481410635432-lMyQjAxMTAwMDEwODExNDgyWj.html.
3. http://www.nytimes.com/2011/05/29/business/29groupon.html?pagewanted=all.
4. http://www.nytimes.com/2011/10/02/business/deal-sites-have-fading-allure-for-merchants.html?_r=2&emc=eta1.
5. Ibid.
6. http://www.retaildoc.com/blog/fallacy-converting-groupon-profitable-customers/.
7. http://www.technologyreview.com/blog/arxiv/27150/.
8. http://www.theglobeandmail.com/report-on-business/careers/management/morning-manager/whats-the-real-impact-of-online-reviews/article2196406/.
9. http://en.wikipedia.org/wiki/Build-A-Bear_Workshop.
10. http://www.buildabear.com/shopping/contents/content.jsp?catId=100003&id=100004.
11. http://www.eurorscgdiscovery.com/clients.html.
12. http://www.mobilemarketer.com/cms/opinion/columns/11061.html.
13. The study that Maclean discusses was based in Europe, but is equally applicable worldwide.
14. http://cityroom.blogs.nytimes.com/2011/05/02/bird-week-welcome-introductio/.

15. http://cityroom.blogs.nytimes.com/2011/05/03/where-do-you-watch-bird-in-new-york-city/.
16. http://www.ted.com/talks/seth_priebatsch_the_game_layer_on_top_of_the_world.html.
17. http://www.ted.com/talks/jane_mcgonigal_gaming_can_make_a_better_world.html.
18. http://www.mobilemarketer.com/cms/opinion/columns/10671 .html.

Chapter 8

1. http://www.nytimes.com/2011/06/25/business/25charity.html?pagewanted=all.
2. Shih, S. (2011, October 18). E-mail interview.
3. http://www.bethkanter.org/switch-data-driven/?utm_source=feedburner&utm_medium=feed&utm_campaign=Feed%3A+bethblog+%28Beth%27s+Blog%29.
4. http://en.wikipedia.org/wiki/WNYC.
5. Colgan, J. (2011, October 14). Personal interview.
6. http://www.nytimes.com/schoolbook/2011/08/30/welcome-to-schoolbook/.
7. http://www.nytimes.com/schoolbook/about/data.
8. http://en.wikipedia.org/wiki/Human_Rights_Campaign#cite_note-wwd-1.
9. http://www.youtube.com/watch?v=ryUX0MT4hZk.
10. http://www.digitalbuzzblog.com/nike-shout-game-day-social-installation/.
11. http://032c.com/2009/never-walk-alone/.

Chapter 9

1. http://en.wikipedia.org/wiki/Aneesh_Chopra.
2. http://radar.oreilly.com/2011/10/data-new-york-city.html.
3. http://www.nytimes.com/2011/08/29/nyregion/wind-and-rain-from-hurricane-irene-lash-new-york.html?pagewanted =all.
4. http://www.nytimes.com/2011/08/29/nyregion/after-the-storm-new-yorkers-complain-about-the-hype.html.
5. http://www.sfgate.com/cgi-bin/article.cgi?f=/c/a/2011/09/14/BAQ41L4PE3.DTL.
6. http://www.mwcog.org/news/press/detail.asp?NEWS_ID=533.
7. http://www.mwcog.org/news/press/detail.asp?NEWS_ID=533.
8. http://www.textually.org/textually/archives/2011/08/029169.htm.
9. Tim Wu. *The Master Switch: The Rise and Fall of Information Empires* (New York: Alfred A Knopf, 2010).
10. http://www.slate.com/articles/technology/technology/2006/05/why_you_should_care_about_network_neutrality.html.
11. Josh Levy, "Net Neutrality: What's Mobile Got to Do With It?," *Save the Internet*, September 30, 2011.
12. http://www.nytimes.com/2007/09/27/us/27verizon.html.
13. Ibid.
14. http://techcrunch.com/2010/12/23/net-neutrality-rules-uncertainty/?icid=tc_tim-wu_art&tag=tim-wu.
15. http://www.slate.com/articles/technology/technology/2006/05/why_you_should_care_about_network_neutrality.html.

INDEX

AARP, 149, 155
Academy for Change, 36
Action [*see* Inspire action (step 3)]
Activism, 23–24, 31–35, 38, 159–165
Adolescents (*see* Teen audiences)
Adoption rate of text messaging by business, 6
Advertising Age, 22, 29
Africa, mobile phone market in, 12–13
Al Qaeda, 32–33
Alexandria Office of Women, 191
Alliance for Climate Education, 109–110, 131
America Online, 10
American Cancer Society Cancer Action Network (ACS CAN), 128–131
Andy Warhol Museum, 133
Apple, 179, 206
Appropriations Committee, 144–145
ARCO Arena, 48–49, 100–101, 113
Ariely, Dan, 88, 101–105
ASPCA, 16, 69
Associated Press, 202
AT&T Mobility, 78
Audience, 14–19, 66–68, 91
    (*See also* Teen audiences)
Auletta, Ken, 12–13

Baltimore Aquarium, 41–43, 64
"Ban Fracking" campaign, 146
Bannon, Ellynne, 89–90
Bean, Chuck, 199
Begin, Meredith, 146
Behavior tracking, 92–100, 189–190
Bell, Alexander Graham, 141–142
Berreby, David, 103
Bias, SMS text messaging, 6–7
Biden, Joe, 175
Bird Week, NYC, 132
Blackbaud, 12

Blank, Jen, 182
Bloomberg, Michael, 58, 166
Blue State Digital, 12
Bond, Jon, 87
Brand news texts, relationship building, 130
Brian Lehrer Show, 166–174
Build-A-Bear Workshop, 122–125
Business adoption rate of text messaging, 6

California Department of Public Health, 17, 187–188, 192
California Poison Control System, 188
California Supreme Court, 175
CAN-SPAM Act, 5
Capital Area Foreclosure Network (CAFN), 198–200
Capital One, 55
Capitol Switchboard, 144
Carnegie Museum/Science Center, 133–134, 137
Celebrate Brooklyn festival, 173
Cell phones (*see* Mobile phones)
Centene, 189–190
Chavez, Hugo, 36
Cheney, Dick, 19
Chevrolet, 31
Chopra, Aneesh, 192
Christian Science Monitor, 13
City Room blog, 132
Clark, Maxine, 122–123
Click-to-call technology, 58
CNET, 31
CNN, 36
Coke, 30
Cole-Lewis, Heather, 99–106
Colgan, Jim, 58, 166–174
College Leadership Seminar, 113
College Mobile Deals, 124–126
Collegiate Leadership Seminar, 51

Commerce and engagement, long-term relationships, 126–134
Common carriage, 201–209
Communications Workers of America (CWA), 78
CompuServe, 10
ComScore, 91
Conversions, data use to increase, 139–157
    connect with users at right time, 148–152
    direct user responses with data, 143–148
    leverage phone-Internet linkages, 141–142
    mobile web, 152–154
    preload user data, 142–143
    target text messages to user's specific needs, 156–157
    user phone numbers, 142–143
Convio, 12
Cost of SMS text messaging, 5, 88–90
Coupons, 116–126
CREDO Mobile, 19, 88
CRM (customer relationship management), mobile, 10–11, 15–17
Crowdsourcing projects, 57–59, 167–173
Customer acquisition, 29–30, 46–47, 119–120

Damon, Matt, 112
Data for one-to-one opportunities, 63–85
    (*See also* Conversions, data use to increase)
DDB Worldwide, 29
"Decade of Thanks," 163
Democracy Now, 107
Democratization of information by Web, 7–14
Denny, 25, 30
Diller, Barry, 9–10, 14
Dinner Tonight campaign, 37–39
Direct Marketing News, 30
Direct user responses, increasing, 143–148
Dog Warden Service's, 201
Dogs, reporting scofflaw owners, 200–201

DoSomething.org, 34–35, 46, 50–51, 79–80, 149, 159–165

Educational health messages, 189–190
Engagement, 18, 126–134
    (*See also* Four steps for one-to-one engagement; Long-term relationships, developing; One-to-one connections)
Engagement texts, relationship building, 130–131
Epidemiologic Reviews, 99, 106
Euro RSCG Discovery, 129
Events, 47–54

Facebook:
    advertising campaign, 84–85
    Carnegie campaign, 133
    DoSomething, 34–35
    functions of, 29
    Gladwell on, 31, 33
    messaging system, 91
    role in activism, 36–39
    social media missed steps, 21–24
    using to engage fans, 46–47
    vitaminwater, 21–23, 25–27
FCC, 206
Food & Water Watch, 146–148, 151
Foreclosure information, 198–200
Forrester, 30
Four steps for one-to-one engagement:
    step 1: one-to-one connections, 41–61
    step 2: one-to-one opportunities, 63–85
    step 3: inspire action, 87–110
    step 4: long-term relationships, developing, 111–137
Foursquare, 134–135
Fox Broadcasting Company, 9, 14
Free airways, 201–209
Free offers, 100–106
Friedman, Tom, 8

Gamification, 134–137
General Motors, 24, 31
Get-out-the-vote campaigns, 89
Ghonim, Wael, 36
Gillette, 11
Gimmik without relationship, 116–123

Gladwell, Malcolm, 31–34, 38
Glass, Ira, 60–61
Glassman, James K., 32
Global System for Mobile
    Communications, 2
Google, 17, 23, 57, 118, 141, 186
Google Maps, 57–59, 132, 169–171
Google's AdSense, 64, 84–85
Government communication
    transformation, 192–196,
    200–201
Grams, Dane, 174–175, 177–178
Greenpeace, 24
Groupon, 115–122, 124–125
Groupon: Why Deep Discounts Are Bad
    for Business (Phibbs), 120–121
Guttierez, Luis, 17

H1N1 influenza flu campaign, 87–188
Hall, Taddy, 22
Harlem Health Promotion Center, 93
Harvard Pilgrim Healthcare,
    189–190
Hayes, Rutherford B., 202
Health information, 92–96, 187–192
Hillebrand, Friedhelm, 2–3, 14, 209
Hochul, Kathy, 74
Hoffman, Reid, 164
Housing information, 198–200
Howard, Alex, 193
Hsieh, Dennys, 25
Hulu, 141
Human Rights campaign (HRC),
    174–178, 188
Humane Society, 126–128, 131

Impulse control, 97–100
In-depth analysis, 80–84
Information *vs.* action, 8–9
Inspire action (step 3), 87–110
    behavioral change, 92–100
    free offers, 100–106
    impulse control, 97–100
    intention, 87
    medical reminders, 92–96
    nudge, 106–110
    one-to-one connections, 42–43,
        59
    reminders and behavioral change,
        92–96
    teenage audiences, 90–92
    text to vote, 88–90

Integrated mobile usage and
    campaigns (*see specific topics*)
Internet:
    information revolution extension,
        7–14
    mobile access of, 185
    mobile phone linkage leverage,
        141–142
    regulation, 186
    repressive regimes and Internet
        empowerment, 35–37
Internet access via mobile, 185–209
    common carriage, 201–209
    as critical tool, 185–187
    free airways, 201–209
    government, 192–196, 200–201
    health information, 187–192
    housing information, 198–200
    transportation, 196–198
Iowa Department of Public Health,
    191
Iraq and Afghanistan Veterans of
    America (IAVA), 44
iTunes, 141

Jarvis, Richard, 3
Jet Blue, 42, 64
Jonas Brothers, 50–51, 79–80, 159

Kanter, Beth, 164
Kapoor, Raj, 164
Keenan, Nancy, 206
Kershaw, 106
Kershaw, Trace, 99, 106
Keywords, 69–70
Kibblesmith, Daniel, 119
Kindle, 141
Kistner, Justin, 29
Krief, Guy, 136–137
Kroc, Ray, 123
Ku Klux Klan, 32
Kundra, Vivek, 192

Labor unions, 77–79
Lancet, 94–95
LGBT issues, Human Rights
    Campaign (HRC), 174–178,
    188
Lind, Seth, 60
LIUNA (Laborers International
    Union of North America),
    78–80

Living Social, 118
Loewenstein, George, 104
Long-term relationships, developing
    (step 4), 111–137
    College Mobile Deals, 124–126
    developing, 43, 59
    gamification, 134–137
    gimmik without relationship,
        116–123
    increased engagement and
        commerce, 126–134
    from single contact point to,
        111–116
    three-party mobile strategy to
        develop, 130–131
Loss leaders, 119–120
Louisville Metro Department of
    Public Health, 97
Loyalty program vs. customer
    acquisition, 29–30
Lublin, Nancy, 161, 164

Maclean, Clive, 129–131
Marcus, Amy Dockser, 94, 104–105
Market research, 10–12, 15–17
Marketing campaigns:
    integrated mobile, 28–29
    pairing existing media plan with
        mobile, 44
    segmentation, 53–54, 69–70
    SMS text messaging, 15–19
    social media metrics, 30–31
    social media missed steps, 21–23
    targeting, 77–80, 156–157
    (See also specific companies)
Marshall, Josh, 10
Martha Stewart Dinners Tonight, 109
Martha Stewart Living (magazine),
    27–28
Martha Stewart Weddings:
    campaign, 97, 104–105, 114, 189
    magazine, 75, 114–115
Mascot Challenge, 55
The Master Switch (Wu), 6, 202
Masterwork Hour (radio show), 166
McCain, John, 176
McDonald's, 123
McGonigal, Jane, 135–136
McKinsey, 11
Media one-to-one connections,
    56–61
MediaConnection.com, 21–22

Medical information, 92–96,
    187–192
Meeker, Mary, 185
Mikulski, Barbara, 144–145
Millenial generation prosumers,
    130–131
Miller, Darcy, 115
Miloh, Tamir, 95–96
Mistakes and lessons learned,
    65–68
MIT, 121
MKTG, 182
Mobile Active, 61
Mobile carriers, 3, 201–209
Mobile Commons, 19, 65, 68, 93, 97,
    124, 146, 207
Mobile communications, 1–20
    extension of Internet information
        revolution, 7–14
    reach of, 13–14
    text messaging as revolutionary,
        1–7
    two-way conversations, 14–19
Mobile data, 63–65, 68–80
Mobile integration (see specific topics)
Mobile Marketer, 129, 136
Mobile phones:
    access to, NY crowdsourcing
        projects, 171
    African market, 12–13
    for effective outreach, 46, 165
    Internet linkage leverage,
        141–142
    SMS text messaging, 3–4
Mobile web conversions, 152–154
Morgan Stanley, 185
Morozov, Evgeny, 35
Mount Sinai Hospital, 95
Movie marketing example, 111–112
MPR (radio), 153
MTA (New York), 197–198
MTA (San Francisco), 197
Mulpuru, Sucharitu, 30
Multiple data fields, 77–80
Murdoch, Rupert, 9
Myspace, 30

Napolitano, Janet, 66
Naral Pro-Choice America,
    205–206
National Coalition for Safer Roads,
    44, 47

National Institutes of Health (NIH), 128
Nestle, 24
The Net Delusion (Morozov), 35
Net neutrality, 203–205
New customer acquisition, 29–30, 46–47, 119–120
New Voters Project, 89
New York (*see* Crowdsourcing projects; WNYC)
New York City Department of Education, 200
New York City Department of Health, 97
New York Office of Emergency Management, 195
New York Presbyterian Hospital, 93
New York Review of Books, 35, 37
New York Times, 10, 56, 95, 103, 118–120, 131–132, 161–162
New Yorker, 9, 31, 102–103, 108
Newsweek, 33
NFL, 149
Nike, 109, 149, 178–183
Nike Shout campaign, 179
Nokia, 3
Nonprofit Roundtable of Greater Washington, 199
Nordstrom, 114
Nudge (Sunstein and Thaler), 88, 106–109
Nudge to inspire action, 106–110
Number of text messages per person, 3–4

O' Reilly Radar, 193–194
Obama, Barack, 17, 50, 67, 72, 79, 108, 176, 192
Offer-based texts, relationship building, 130
Office of Information and Regulatory Affairs, 108
Old media, and new ways to engage, 56
One-to-one communication transformations, 185–209
common carriage, 201–209
as critical tool, 185–187
government, 192–196, 200–201
health information, 187–192
housing information, 198–200
transportation, 196–198

One-to-one company transformations, 159–184
DoSomething, 159–165
Human Rights Campaign (HRC), 174–178, 188
Nike, 178–183
WNYC, 166–174, 195
One-to-one connections (step 1), 41–61
building, 42, 59
developing long-term relationships, 43, 59
discover opportunities, 42, 59
for events, 47–54
four steps, 41–43
inspire action, 42–43, 59
media, 56–61
social media missed steps, 37–38
universal, 44–47
viral, 54–56
One-to-one opportunities (step 2), 63–85
data use for in-depth analysis, 80–84
discovering, 42, 59
know your audience, 66–68
mistakes and what it can teach you, 65–68
mobile data for, 63–65
multiple data for targeting users, 77–50
text messaging *vs.* contextual advertisement, 84–85
types of mobile data, 68–80
Online Journalism Award, 170
Online News Association, 170
Opinionway Research, 29
Organizing for America (OFA), 72–75, 77

Papa John's, 124
Papworth, Neil, 2–3
Parker, Mark, 179
Parking, 196–197
Past actions, capturing user, 76
Paul, Weiss, Rifkind, Wharton & Garrison LLP, 7
PediatricSuperSite, 92
Penn Relays, Nike, 179–182
Personal connections (*see* One-to-one connections)
Pets, reporting scofflaw owners, 200–201

Pew poll, 91
Phibbs, Bob, 120–121
Philbin, Bob, 164
Phone numbers, capturing, 68, 142–143
Pihkonen, Riku, 3
Pizza Hut, 124–125
Planned Parenthood Federation of America (PPFA), 191
Plow maps, crowdsourced, 57–59, 169–171
Powell, Colin, 8, 10, 12
Power Balance Pavilion, 48
Predictably Irrational (Ariely), 88, 103
Preloaded user data, 142–143
Priesbatsch, Seth, 135
Proctor & Gamble, 11
Prodigy, 10
Project Masiluleke, 99
Project STAY (Services to Assist Youth), 93
Prosumers, 130–131
Public Radio International (PRI), 76–77

Qdoba, 124
QR codes, 52–53
Radio, 56–61, 76–77
  (*See also* WNYC)
Real estate foreclosures, 198–200
Reality is Broken: Why Games Make Us Better (McGonigal), 135–136
Reform Immigration For America, 16–18, 34, 43, 55, 65–69, 76, 80–84, 144
Reform Immigration with Your Cell Phone, 80–82
Regimes, Internet empowerment and, 35–37
Reiskin, Ed, 197
Relationships (*see* Long-term relationships, developing; One-to-one connections)
Reminders and behavioral change, 92–96
Responses and response rates, 80–84, 143–148
Robertson, Rebecca, 27

Sacramento Kings, 48–51, 64, 100–101, 113, 156–157
Salesforce.com, 10–12, 23, 207

Salsa, 12
San Francisco Chronicle, 197
Sanchez, Michael, 159
Sand, Peggy, 200
Save Darfur Coalition, 33
Save the Internet Coalition, 204–205
Save the Music Campaign, 46, 79
Scanning QR codes, 52–53
Scavenger hunts, 133–134, 162–163
Schmidt, Eric, 23, 34, 71, 207
SchoolBook, 171–172
Schultz, Howard, 123
SCVNGR, 135
Segmentation, 53–54, 69–70
Sexual health information, 190–191
SFpark, 196–197
Sharkey, Kevin, 27
Shedd Aquarium, 46
Shih, Stephanie, 161–162, 164–165
Shue, Andrew, 159
Sierra Club, 19
Single contact point, 111–116
Skittles, 24
Skype, 39, 141
Slate (magazine), 203, 208
SMS (short message service)
  bridge across the digital divide, 4–5
  business adoption rate, 6
  cost of, 5
  engagement, 18
  length of message, 2
  market research, 10–11, 15–17
  marketing campaigns, 15–19
  on mobile phones, 3–4
  number per person, 3–4
  origins of, 2–3
  spam protections, 5
  suspicions and biases, 6–7
  as universally available, 4
Snowmaps, crowdsourced, 57–59, 169–171
Social media, 21–39
  activism, 31–35, 38
  broad and one-to-one connections, 37–38
  driving mobile engagement, 46–47
  Facebook, 21–24
  loyalty program *vs.* customer acquisition, 29–30
  missed opportunity of data leverage, 24–31

societal good, 35–37
vs. traditional connection, 23–24
well-considered goals, 24–31
Societal good, 35–37
Spam protections, 5
St. Jude Children's Research Hospital, 51–54, 113–114
Starbucks, 123
Sterne, Rachel, 193–194
Stewart, Martha, 27–28, 37–39, 56
Stockwell, Melissa, 92
Stonyfield Farm, 43
Stop Global Warming Virtual March, 33–34
Student PIRG, 89
Summer Museum Adventure, 133
Sundance Film Festival, 75, 77
Sunstein, Cass, 88, 106–109
Suspicions, SMS text messaging, 6–7
SUV crowdsourcing, WNYC, 167–168
Suxorz, 25

The Takeaway (news show), 171
Talking Points Memo, 10
Targeting users, 77–80, 156–157
Teach for America, 144–145
TechCrunch blog, 206
Technology Review, 120
TED and TEDX conferences, 134–135
Teen audiences:
DoSomething, 159–165
inspire action, 90–92
Internet access via mobile, 190–191
Nike Penn Relays, 179–182
Teens for Jeans, 160
Telephone Consumer Protection Act, 5
Television viewing by children, 189–190
Text message invention, 209
(*See also* SMS; *specific topics*)
"Text Messaging as a Tool for Behavior Change" (Cole-Lewis and Kershaw), 99
Tezanos, Melisa, 31
Thaler, Richard H., 88, 106

ThePoint, 117
This American Life (radio show), 59–60
ThumbWars, 160
Time and dates, 75–76, 148–152
Transportation, 196–198
Tri Delta Fraternity, 51
Twitter, 25, 35–36, 46–47
Two-way conversations, 14–19

Universal availability of text messaging, 4, 44–47
Upstream, 136
U.S. State Department, 176
UWC Mixed Martial Arts, 101

Van Hollen, Chris, 144–145
Verizon, 186, 205
VH1, 46, 50, 79
Viral marketing, 54–56
Vitaminwater, 21, 23, 25–27
Volunteering (*see* Inspire action)
Von Furstenburg, Diane, 9
Voting, 88–90, 169

Wall Street Journal, 94, 104–105, 117–118
Weather events, 57–59, 169–172, 193–196
Webtrends, 29
Western Union, 202
White House, 65, 108, 146–147, 165
Wikipedia, 43–44, 103, 116–117
With, Aaron, 118
WNYC (radio), 56–57, 109, 132, 166–174, 194–196
Woolworth, 31–32
Working Assets (now CREDO Mobile), 88
World Health Organization, 94
The World (radio show), 76–77
The World Is Flat (Friedman), 8
Wu, Tim, 6, 202–204, 206, 208

Yahoo News, 56
Yelp, 121–122

032C (magazine), 179
Zip code of user, 71–72
Zuckerberg, Mark, 36, 91, 207

ABOUT THE AUTHORS

Jed Alpert, cofounded and is the chief executive officer of Mobile Commons. He is considered one of the foremost authorities on mobile communications strategy, and he and his work have been featured in the *New York Times*, the *Wall Street Journal*, the *Washington Post*, the *New Yorker*, *Fast Company*, MSNBC, and many more. He has guest lectured at the Kennedy School of Government and New York University and has recently been a featured speaker at the Nonick International Conference on Internet Trends, the Nonprofit Technology Conference, the National Conference on Media Reform, and more. Additionally, he is a frequent participant in Aspen Institute forums and Ford Foundation events.

Stephen Fishbach heads up marketing and communications for Mobile Commons. Before joining Mobile Commons, Stephen worked as a strategist for big and small media companies, with clients ranging from Epic Records to Ford Motors. Stephen also helped launch mtvU, MTV's college television channel. Campaigns Stephen has worked on have won Emmy Awards, a Peabody Award, and numerous Beacon Awards. AdWeek selected the HBO Voyeur campaign, for which Stephen served as strategist, as one of the 10 best digital campaigns of the decade. Stephen has a BA in English from Yale University and writes a weekly blog on *Survivor* for People.com.

DATE DUE	RETURNED